Help! I'm A New Mom

A First-Time Mother's Guide to Mastering Newborn Care and Postpartum Recovery

Jocelyn Goodwin

Contents

How To Get The Most Out Of This Book

For the glowing new mom or mom-to-be, I've created two free bonuses to save you money, time, and headaches. These bonuses are updated in real-time and change as new products and resources become available.

I highly recommend you sign up now to get the most out of this book. You can do that by going to the link below.

www.thefirst12months.com/#bonusnewmom

Free Bonus #1: Postpartum Essentials for New Moms: Tried and tested products to help you recover and thrive after labor.

Free Bonus #2: Must-Have Items for Every Baby: The ultimate list of everything you need for your newborn, including some specific brands and products I love.

Free Bonus #3: My Favorite Postpartum Recipes: Printable PDF that includes healing soups, hydrating drinks, lactation cookies and more.

To get your bonuses, go to:

www.thefirst12months.com/#bonusnewmom

Foreword

By Sarah Schulze

New parenthood is an experience unlike any other. The overwhelming love, exhaustion, adoration, frustration, and awe experienced – and sometimes cycled through in rapid succession – are enough to humble even the most prepared and educated individuals. Suddenly, mundane things you've never even thought about seem confusing, overwhelming, or even alarming. You'll find yourself wondering about poop color, baby sneezes, and... what *is* that oozing out of the umbilical cord?

Perhaps the only thing more overwhelming than actually caring for your new family member is sorting through the mountains of information on how best to do it. There is so much to learn about normal infant growth and development, and there are even more *opinions* about how your every decision stands to affect your child for the rest of their life. Many new parents find themselves paralyzed with the fear of making a "wrong" choice or doing something incorrectly.

Even as a pediatric nurse practitioner and lactation counselor with over a decade of experience, I found myself exhausted and overwhelmed by the enormous chasm between my expectations and the reality of actually bringing a baby home. When navigating parenthood, there is a certain type of assuredness and wisdom that can only be gained through experience, and Jocelyn's book offers a wonderful glimpse into the easy confidence of someone who has been there.

Help! I'm a New Mom provides a refreshing combination of realistic and empathetic advice, while following safe and evidence-based guidelines for everything from breastfeeding to infant sleep, and more! Jocelyn astutely notes the differences between what modern parenting advice often looks like and what babies actually need from a simple, biological standpoint.

Too often, modern parenting guides have complicated formulas for how to "schedule" your baby and make them sleep, eat, or even poop in a very specific routine, leading to exasperated parents pouring their precious energy into an unattainable goal. *Help! I'm a New Mom* takes a wonderfully laid-back and baby-centered approach, gently reminding parents that each baby is unique and there is no one-size-fits-all secret to successful parenting.

Having survived the early days with my own three children and witnessed every parenting style imaginable in my career, I feel confident saying that much of what new parents fret about in those first few months has nothing to do with whether or not they have a "good baby" or are a "good parent," but is fueled by unmet expectations and misguided advice about how babies should be behaving, eating, or sleeping. Time and time again, I see parents come into the clinic with their second, third, or fourth babies, and things are so much easier! This isn't because subsequent babies are somehow "better;" it is because the parents now have the experience and confidence needed to navigate the newborn phase more comfortably.

I have often tried to harness this perspective and convey it to new parents, reassuring them that what they are going through is a universal and completely normal experience! This book does just that, offering an informative, calming, and relatable guide that new parents can return to again and again. As a pediatric professional and a mother, I highly recommend *Help! I'm a New Mom* to any expectant parent.

Sarah Schulze CPNP

Sarah Schulze MSN, APRN, APRN, CPNP, CLC,
*Pediatric Nurse Practitioner, Certified
Lactation Counselor*

You're Going to Be a Mom!

Every time I meet a first-time mom, I get super excited! That's because it's their first experience, and "firsts" always hold a special place in your heart. Like your first day of school, your first solo trip, or your first day at a new job.

Firsts come with butterflies and giddiness, but also excitement and hope. Firsts are what we prepare for. We put in all our effort and build up expectations that the experience will be flawless.

Unfortunately, firsts also come with intense pressure to fit into a mold or behave a certain way, and it often feels like you're building the plane while flying it.

You may have spent years imagining what it will be like to be a mom or deciding what kind of mom you'll be, but I need you to do me a favor. Take the expectations you have about motherhood and throw them out. If there's a window near you, go ahead and toss them out there so you're not tempted to pick them up again.

You're Going to Be a Mom!

If you aim for perfection and begin this journey with fixed ideas, you're just setting yourself up for failure. Soon, you'll begin to find motherhood exhausting and daunting. Try your best to take every day as it comes because motherhood is beautiful, challenging, and unpredictable.

The only perfect parents that exist are the ones who don't have kids yet! You may have heard other people talk about what they would never do or allow as a parent. You might even have said it yourself. It's certainly simpler to be a perfect parent before the baby arrives, but your experience as a new mom may look nothing like you expected, and that's okay. It's easy to be ideological and certain of your ideas before you're actually in uncharted territory as a new mom, and you're allowed to change your mind.

Once you ditch the idea of having a perfect journey into motherhood and accept that it's okay not to know everything, you'll find yourself laughing and having fun. And the best part is, you are going to be a great mom!

Whether you picked this book up because you are getting ready to have a baby or because you've recently given birth, I want you to know what is normal. Every baby is different, but if you know what normal newborn behavior is and what normal postpartum recovery is like, you're less likely to freak out when something unexpected happens.

As a new mom, I quickly discovered that there's a big gap between what your pediatrician knows and what you know as a parent. Although I frantically read every pregnancy and newborn book I could get my hands on and got sucked into the black hole we call the internet, I still felt completely lost and naive when it came to caring for my newborn.

No one told me that I would be up all night with them on the second and third night after giving birth. No one told me that newborn skin wouldn't look like perfect baby skin. And definitely, no one told me that breastfeeding would be unbelievably difficult and wouldn't just come naturally.

This book is about preparing you for the first few months of your baby's life. Especially as a new mom, knowledge is power. Many of us spend too much time focusing on pregnancy and birth, and neglect the time after giving birth, leaving us unprepared for the postpartum period. When you know what is normal and you know what to expect, you're empowered to make the best decisions for your family.

The best way to use this book is to read it cover to cover and then refer back to it when needed. You're not going to remember everything you read, so I've divided it into easy-to-read chapters, organized by topics. For example, if you're trying to transition your baby to a bottle, you can revisit Chapter 5 on No-Nonsense Bottle-feeding. If you're struggling to get your baby to sleep, go back to Chapter 6 on the A, B, Zzzz of Sleep. Parenting can be lonely at times, so I hope it helps you feel like you're not alone and provides you with guidance when you don't know what to do.

When discussing baby behavior, I like to look back to how things were done before "modern society," as I think humans haven't really evolved much since those times. Things like sleep training and feeding schedules are relatively new and still aren't the norm in many parts of the world. A lot of our modern ideas around babies contradict what we have done for centuries and our biological wiring as mammals. Trusting your instincts is usually a good idea; they're there for a reason.

In this book, I have included everything I wish I'd known as a first-time mom so you have a one-stop shop that will guide you through the first 6 months with your little one. It's my hope that after reading this book, you'll know that every parent, even the ones who look like they have it all together, are trying to figure their new world out too. Parenting can be messy and confusing, and adjusting to a life where someone needs you 24/7 can be overwhelming. While I can't promise much, I do promise that motherhood is one wild and crazy ride!

So grab a cup of decaf or maybe a herbal tea. Let's go through the journey of motherhood together. I know you're going to be great!

1
Preparing for the Big Day

There it is – that little pink line. With it comes a flood of emotions. You might feel excitement, overwhelming joy, and perhaps a bit of panic. It's reassuring that you have 9 months to prepare for motherhood, but those 9 months will go by more quickly than you expect.

At the beginning of your pregnancy, there's no reason to stress yourself out and get everything ready for the baby right away, but you'll soon start feeling the "nesting instinct" kicking in.

As a general rule of thumb, it's best to be ready by 6 weeks before your due date, in case your little one is excited to get this party started early. This 6 week cushion means you're not scrambling at the last minute if you go into labor early.

When it comes to preparing yourself and your household for your little one, communication is key. Don't neglect the difficult conversations, especially if you and your partner are of different religions or have major cultural differences. For example, if you are planning on having a religious ceremony, such as a baptism, you should talk about this well in advance so it can be planned.

It's easy to feel overwhelmed by the decision-making process, but the more decisions you can make in advance, the less time you'll have to spend thinking about them after the birth.

Decisions on How You'll Give Birth

When it comes to giving birth, having a plan is crucial, but try to be flexible as well. Just like your baby's due date, birth is unpredictable, and things may not go exactly as planned. Whether you're preparing for an unmedicated birth or having an epidural, a birth class is a great way to learn what to expect.

In most birth classes, you'll learn about different birthing positions and the options you'll have in labor. Some birth classes can be as long as 12 weeks, and they often fill up quickly, so try looking for one by the second trimester. In your class, you'll have an opportunity to ask questions, learn about the birthing process, and meet other couples who are also having a baby. When you're a first-time mom, you may not know anyone else with kids yet, and sometimes connections like these can lead to life-long friendships.

No matter what kind of birth you plan on having, being informed allows you to make the best decision for you and your baby. If possible, have your partner attend a birthing class with you. There may come a time when your partner needs to advocate for you during labor, so being involved can be helpful.

Decisions at the Hospital

There are some decisions that won't affect you until you get home, and there are other decisions you'll need to make before leaving the hospital. If you're having a boy, for example, you'll want to have a discussion about circumcision prior to having your baby. This decision is huge for your baby boy, and you won't necessarily have the energy or strength to make a thoughtful decision right after birth. Like any medical decision, this isn't one you want to make without weighing the pros and cons.

Some other decisions that will affect your baby after birth are whether you'll store cord blood and what you'll do with your placenta. Having the hospital dispose of your placenta is certainly an option, but many moms choose to encapsulate their placenta, which has to be arranged in advance.

Without complications, your hospital stay may be only 24 to 48 hours, but if you have a c-section or there are any health concerns with you or your baby, your stay could end up being longer. It's therefore important to think about things like who will care for your pets and what additional support you might need when you return home.

Let's say you're free to leave the hospital at 8 p.m. on a Saturday. Have you prepared freezer meals so that you have something to eat once you get home? Will you pick something up on the way? Or do you have family and friends who have offered to cook for you the first few days after coming home? You will be hyper focused on feeding your baby during this time, but be sure you and your partner are taken care of as well.

Decisions on How You'll Feed Your Baby

One of the biggest decisions to make before your baby is born is how you want to feed them. There are pros and cons to both breastfeeding and formula feeding, just like there are for most things in motherhood. Having some basic knowledge about both options, what you are going to need, and what kind of support you'll require postpartum is essential.

Sometimes, parents decide they want to breastfeed, but then encounter problems that mean they have to swap to bottle-feeding. It's a good idea to have some equipment on hand in

3

case this happens to you, so you're prepared if things don't go to plan.

Decisions on Household Responsibilities & Baby Care

It might be difficult to think about while you're still pregnant, but this is the best time to discuss what will happen after the baby arrives. Talk about how you'll handle paternity and maternity leave so you don't have to stress about it later. Will your partner take time off to help you and spend time with your new family? Will you be returning to work after the baby comes or staying at home permanently? Your decision doesn't have to be set in stone, but having a plan is important.

You also may want to have a discussion with your partner and anyone else in your support system about the expectations for caring for yourself and the little one. It's worth thinking about who will be responsible for which household responsibilities and baby duties during the first few weeks. Consider whether your partner will help with diaper changes or nighttime feedings. Even if this seems obvious to you, talk to your partner to make sure you're on the same page.

It's imperative that you focus on recovering during this time (more on that later!), so make sure your partner is aware that you won't be able to do basic household tasks at first, such as laundry or dishes. Your job is to rest and snuggle with your baby. If possible, think about asking a trusted friend or family member to come over and help with cleaning or cooking.

Decisions on Visitors After Birth

Talking about visitors after birth can be a touchy subject for some friends and family. Although many people will want to come and meet your bundle of joy, remember to set clear boundaries and expectations. You shouldn't feel pressured to entertain or have people over until you're comfortable. We'll look at this more in the section on postpartum recovery, but be aware that even if you think you'll want people over right away, you don't know how you'll be feeling after the birth. There's nothing wrong with making it clear that you're not sure when you'll want visitors, and politely asking friends and family not to show up unannounced.

No matter what kind of birth you have, it's pretty much guaranteed that you'll be exhausted, sore, and potentially leaking milk. Let everyone in your circle know you'll tell them when you're ready, and ask them to be respectful of that boundary. It may be helpful to send out a text or email to those closest to you, letting them know what your plans for visitors are before the baby comes.

Prepare Yourself Mentally

It's essential to care for yourself as well as your baby during pregnancy and postpartum. Managing your stress is crucial to your well-being, but most moms will tell you that that's easier said than done. One way to help yourself relax is to learn a deep breathing exercise.

Here is my go-to breathing exercise. First, breathe in for 7 seconds, and then breathe out for 11. It may not sound like much, but giving yourself a few minutes to breathe and pause can relieve some of the stress you're feeling.

It also may be helpful to have a mantra for birth, postpartum, or any time you feel stressed during the pregnancy. A mantra is simply a positive thought you repeat to yourself to improve your mindset. When you find yourself overwhelmed during the birth, you might say:

- "I trust my body to deliver my baby."
- "I am strong and capable of delivering my baby."

If you are worried or overwhelmed during the postpartum period, you might try:

- "I trust my instincts."
- "One step at a time."
- "This is difficult, but everything will be okay."
- "I'm doing the best I can."

Write your mantra somewhere that you will see it frequently throughout the day. It can help change your mindset and gives you something to focus on when you feel yourself worrying about your circumstances.

Throughout labor and the postpartum period, try your best to go with the flow. You may be the kind of person who doesn't do well without structure and routine, but you're going to have to cope with some flexibility, particularly during the first 6-12 weeks postpartum. Your schedule will revolve around your baby. If you have a hard time going with the flow, try focusing on some of the things that you can control, such as what you're eating or how you spend your time while the baby naps.

Once the baby comes, your routine will look very different, and that's okay. For a while, it's going to seem like your whole world has been turned upside down, because it has! You're likely not going to get much sleep at first, and you might have to get used to napping during the day while your baby naps.

Your meal times will change, and might be unpredictable. In the early days of motherhood, there'll be days when you can't remember the last time you took a shower or washed your face. Don't despair; before you know it, you'll be out of the newborn phase, and your routine will change again. Enjoy all the newborn snuggles while you can!

Get the Baby Gear Ready

One of the most exciting parts of preparing for your baby is purchasing all the baby gear and setting up a registry – but the number of options out there can quickly become overwhelming.

When it comes to baby gear, focus on the necessities. It's tempting to register for everything and panic over all the items you feel like you need. However, no matter how cute all of the baby gear is, a lot of it is unnecessary, especially in the early days. Don't worry if you don't have everything off your registry by the time the baby comes. As long as you have the necessities, you'll have plenty of time to get the rest.

What you should have right away:

- A car seat
- A safe place for the baby to sleep, including a crib, mattress, mattress protector, and fitted sheets
- A changing station, including diapers, wipes, and diaper rash cream
- Basic hygienic and safety items, such as a first aid kit, nail clippers, baby soap, an infant thermometer, saline spray, and a nasal suction device
- Feeding supplies, including burp cloths and bottles
- A night light

When you've imagined bringing your baby home, you've probably imagined exactly what outfit they'll be wearing, but remember that most of your time will be spent at home during the first few weeks, and you'll likely only be leaving the house for doctors appointments. Pick one special outfit for your baby to wear home from the hospital, and then opt for practical baby clothes.

How many baby outfits you need depends on how often you'll do laundry. If you plan on doing laundry once a week, it will be beneficial for you to have:

- 10-14 bodysuits or rompers (depending on weather)
- 3-5 pairs of pants
- 8 pajamas (sleepers, gowns or onesies)
- 2 hats (4 hats if you live in a cold climate and go outside frequently)
- 3 swaddle blankets
- 2-7 pairs of socks (depending on weather)

It's best to underestimate how frequently you'll do laundry, since it's easier to be on top of tasks like this before you have a newborn baby.

Any clothing that you get in a newborn size will usually fit babies up to 8 pounds. Some newborns will outgrow this size in several weeks, so make sure you purchase some of each of the above items in size 0-3, which is intended for weights up to 13 pounds.

It is also important to pay attention to the material of clothing you are purchasing. The best materials for baby clothing are natural materials that can breathe, such as cotton. Polyester and other synthetic materials can make your baby feel damp and may irritate the skin.

In addition to the necessary baby gear, there are some things that aren't necessary, but may make your life easier, including:

- A baby monitor
- A baby carrier
- A stroller
- A white noise machine
- A rocker, bouncer, or swing
- Some pacifiers

- A glider or rocking chair
- Blackout curtains
- Bedtime books

Don't Forget Gear for Yourself

Most moms fill their baby registry with items for the baby, but it's helpful to add some items for yourself as well! When you're coming home from the hospital, you'll be glad you stocked up on maxi pads, adult diapers, nipple cream, and nursing pads. The hospital will typically provide a peri bottle (a squirt bottle for cleaning the area between your vagina and anus), but there are brands that sell better quality versions if you'd prefer to buy your own.

As far as clothing for yourself, make sure you have lots of loose clothing and loose high waisted underwear. You won't fit into your pre-pregnancy clothing (or underwear!) for a while, and you'll want to be as comfortable as possible. Dark clothing is best for new moms since there are bound to be spills and leaks, from both you and your baby.

If you plan on breastfeeding, invest in some breastfeeding clothing. This can include a breastfeeding bra that easily allows you to remove one strap, a pullover wrap, or tops that allow easy access to the breast.

Go to www.thefirst12months.com/#bonusnewmom to see my most recent and up-to-date recommendations for all these items and more.

To-do List

Making a to-do list is a great way to stay on top of everything you'll need to accomplish before the baby comes, so let's check out what you might put on the list.

Jocelyn Goodwin

Install the Car Seat and Set up the Crib

The car seat is one of the first things you'll need before you bring your baby home. You won't be able to leave the hospital without it. However, you don't want to install your car seat too early in case of a car accident. Even if the baby isn't in the car seat, it will no longer be safe to use after an accident, so wait until you're around 35 weeks along.

You will also need to get your crib or bassinet set up and ready so your baby has a safe place to sleep as soon as you return home.

Prepare Some Meals

When you first get home from the hospital, you and your partner will be exhausted and definitely won't want to cook, so preparing freezer meals ahead of time can be a huge help. The easiest way to do this is to double some of the recipes you're already using and then freeze them. If you're feeling adventurous, you can also look for postnatal soup recipes, lactation cookies, or anything else that may be comforting to you.

If you're not the cooking type, see if your support system can prepare freezer meals for you, or take turns dropping off meals over the first few weeks. You may also plan to have food delivered through a food delivery service. When you've got a new baby, you don't want to worry about what's for dinner!

Wash Your Baby Clothes

Since newborns have sensitive skin, wash their clothes before they wear them to get rid of any potential irritants. You don't need to wash all your baby's clothes at once, but launder enough for at least the first week. Remember, your newborn might have lots of spills and diaper changes, so plan on them needing several new outfits a day.

Pack Your Hospital Bag

Packing your hospital bag is one of the top priorities for your to-do list! There may be some extra items you decide to pack, but here are the essentials:

- Photo ID, insurance information, birth plan, and any other hospital forms
- Daily medication
- Maxi pads or adult diapers (they will also offer these in the hospital)
- A nursing bra and nipple cream if you plan on breastfeeding
- Your own pillow
- Comfortable underwear
- Big, comfy clothes
- A robe
- Socks and/or slippers
- A blanket for the baby
- Onesies in two sizes; it's a good idea to bring a newborn size and 0-3 months since you don't know how big your baby will be
- Your own toiletries
- Your phone and charger
- Snacks
- Books, magazines, and other entertainment

You should also think about whether you need things like hair ties and glasses/contacts. Remember that you may be in hospital for some time if you have a long or complicated labor, so it's better to over-prepare.

Get Recovery Gear Ready

Jocelyn Goodwin

You are likely to be sore when you return from the hospital, so it's worth getting some recovery gear ready, such as ice packs or postpartum pads. Some options for recovery are:

- Buying frozen peas
- Filling a condom with water, tying the end, and freezing it
- Making your own postpartum padsicles

Padsicle recipe:

1. Take a thick maxi pad or reusable cloth pad
2. Soak it in witch hazel
3. Place it in a ziplock bag (you can fold it in half if necessary)
4. Freeze
5. Place it in your underwear.

This is just another quick step that you'll be glad you took care of before labor when your breasts and/or vagina are super uncomfortable and you want something cold to put on them.

Sign Yourself up for a Mommy Class

I would highly recommend signing yourself up for a mommy class for 4-6 weeks after birth. You probably won't want to attend one right away, but after a while, you might be eager for some social interactions. If by 4-6 weeks, you don't feel like going, that's okay, but a mommy class can be a safe place where others understand what you're going through. It can ease some of the emotional burdens you may be carrying and make you feel supported.

It can also ease you into getting out of the house more. The first social outing might be scary, but you'll feel better after interacting with other moms.

Schedule a Newborn Session

If you plan to have a newborn photography session for your little one, schedule it now. They often fill up fast, and you'll have plenty of other things to think about after the birth.

Many of the above tasks are fun to think about, but there are also some items on your to-do list that are not as exciting. That said, you'll still be glad you took care of them before the baby arrived!

Baby-Proof the House

You don't need to worry about baby gates, outlets, or cabinets right away since your baby won't usually be crawling for at least 6 months, but you should make sure that your smoke detectors, carbon monoxide detectors, and fire extinguishers are working.

Find a Pediatrician

Most pediatricians will want to see your baby just a few days after the birth, so make sure you find a pediatrician beforehand. Ask a friend for a recommendation if you're looking for one in your area, and check with your insurance to ensure they're in your network.

Check With Health Insurance

Most health insurance companies have newborn care that covers your baby for a period of time, typically 30 days, after the birth. Give them a call to find out what the newborn care covers, how to add your baby to the insurance, and if there's anything else you need to do to ensure your baby has coverage.

Get Breastfeeding Help

Breastfeeding is a challenge! However, you can do it successfully with the right support. If you plan on breastfeeding, identify who you'll reach out to for support ahead of time. This might include a lactation specialist, a friend who has experience, or a breastfeeding group, such as La Leche League, in your area.

Waiting until the last minute to find support can make your breastfeeding journey harder.

You can also build confidence in yourself by hand expressing colostrum, starting at 36 weeks. Instructions on how to hand express can be found in Chapter 4.

If you plan on breastfeeding but have flat or inverted nipples, consider wearing nipple formers or breast shells from 32 weeks. Breast shells are soft, flexible discs that fit discreetly inside your bra and place gentle pressure on your nipples to help draw them out. Try wearing them for 5-15 minutes a day at first, and build up.

Pick Your Emergency Contacts

If anything goes wrong, it's crucial to have people who can watch your baby in an emergency. Choose at least two in case one isn't available.

Calculate Your Expenses

You don't need to panic about all the expenses of a child from birth until college, but it's beneficial to at least be prepared for the first year. It's estimated that from birth to age one in 2022, a baby costs $15,775. To calculate your own expenses, you can visit:

https://www.babycenter.com/baby-cost-calculator

Be Excited!

Every stress and worry you may have now will disappear the moment you lay eyes on your baby for the first time. Even though it's easier said than done, try not to focus on what you can't control. Be excited! Soon, your little one will be in your arms.

2

Ouch! Healing and Recovery After Birth

Before we talk about the challenging and blissful first week with your newborn, there's something else we need to discuss. It's important to know what your body will go through during the first 6 weeks postpartum. Many moms spend so much time preparing to take care of their little ones that they forget to make a plan for taking care of themselves, and the recovery part is swept under the rug.

Caring for yourself postpartum isn't a luxury; it's a necessity. To heal properly and care for your baby, you must take care of yourself. The best way to have a healthy baby is to have a healthy mom. Even more importantly, *you matter!*

Everyone, including your family and friends, will likely be focused on your baby after birth. They'll ask if they can come over, how the baby is doing, and whether they can hold it. Although they mean well, it might feel like your experience and healing isn't important. Whether your support system recognizes it or not, you are the one who gave birth, and you have to prioritize your healing, recovery, and overall well-being. With that in mind, let's get into what postpartum recovery looks like.

Postpartum Recovery

Birth is an incredible process, and even though the recovery part isn't easy, your bundle of joy will make it all worthwhile. Postpartum recovery isn't something to panic about, but you need to know what to expect. There are many joyful moments during the postpartum period, but there are many challenging ones as well, so let's be real about how you might feel postpartum.

After birth, your entire vagina and pelvic region will be uncomfortable and swollen, so even though you need to lie down or sit down to recover, expect sitting to be uncomfortable and painful for a while. Whether you choose to breastfeed or not, your body prepares to feed your baby, so your breast, nipples, and areolas will be sore. Once your milk comes in, your breasts will be uncomfortable or possibly painful until your milk supply adjusts. After the euphoria of birth wears off, you'll realize your body has been through a lot and you'll start to feel it physically.

Your uterus will need time to shrink after birth, and your organs will need time to go back to their normal places. If you had a vaginal birth with any tearing, you might have stitches that need to heal, and if you had a c-section, you'll be recovering from major surgery. On top of the physical pain and discomfort you may be feeling, you will also be tired and often overwhelmed by trying to figure out how to be a mom.

All of this may seem like a lot, and it is! Your body has to go through a lot to give birth. For many moms, recovery may be the hardest part, but like any recovery process, you'll start to feel a little better each day.

The postpartum period is also known as postnatal care, or sometimes, the 4th trimester. This period is divided into three phases:[1]

Initial Postpartum Phase: Lasts for 6-19 Hours After Childbirth

During this first phase, if you had a hospital birth, you will likely still be there. While you're in the hospital, they'll monitor your heart rate, blood pressure, oxygen, and vaginal bleeding before sending you home.

Subacute Postpartum Phase: Lasts for Around 6 Weeks

This phase is often the most difficult. It's when your body is recovering and changing the most. Your hormones are adjusting to pre-pregnancy levels, so sadness, guilt, and loss of interest are normal. Many women find they are emotional during this time.

You will also likely have less energy as your body continues to recover and learns to cope with less sleep. You might notice a change in your appetite as your body regulates and balances your milk production. Vaginal bleeding should also start to subside. Your first few weeks will likely look something like this:

Week 1: You should be in bed!

Week 2: You'll probably still be in bed recovering, but you might also make your way to the couch

Week 3: You'll probably spend most of your time on the couch

Accepting that you won't be able to do a lot at first can be a challenge for many moms, but the most productive thing you can do during this time is rest!

Delayed Postpartum Phase: Lasts for Around 6-8 Months

During this last part of the postpartum phase, you can expect to see more gradual changes in your body, including the restoration of your muscle tone and connective tissue. This is also a time when some women's periods will return, depending on if they are breastfeeding.

Uterine Cramping

After you give birth, your uterus contracts to return to its pre-pregnancy size, and your blood vessels narrow to prevent you from losing too much blood. When your baby is born, your uterus weighs approximately 2.5 pounds, but it decreases to just 2 ounces by 6 weeks postpartum.[2]

Your uterus contracting after birth can be painful for a couple of weeks. The most intense pain is usually during days 2 and 3 after birth, but it can last up to 2 weeks. If you're breastfeeding, you might notice strong contractions during breastfeeding; that's normal. The oxytocin that is released during breastfeeding encourages contractions, which are your body's natural way of returning your uterus to its proper size.[3]

To help relieve some of the pain, pee often, even if you don't feel like you have to go. A full bladder prevents the uterus from fully contracting and slows down the process.[4]

See a doctor if: you have intense pain in your lower belly or pain that extends to your lower back or side. You should also see a doctor if you have cramping that doesn't ease up after a few days.[5]

Postpartum Bleeding

Postpartum bleeding is called lochia, and it happens regardless of what kind of birth you have. It should start as dark red in color, almost like a heavy period, and it may include some blood clots. Over the first couple weeks, the lochia will go from a brownish-pinkish color to a creamy white/yellow discharge, like you might see at the end of your period.[6]

With postpartum bleeding, the flow can last up to 6 weeks. You can expect to wear maxi pads or adult diapers for the first few weeks. It may seem embarrassing to wear adult diapers, but they're usually easier and more comfortable than wearing a heavy-duty pad all day. There's no shame in doing what's most comfortable during recovery. No matter what the lochia flow is like, don't wear tampons until at least 6 weeks!

If you choose to wear pads, be prepared to change them every few hours, and consider wearing one in the front and one in the back to prevent leaks. It's also normal to have a gush of extra blood while your uterus is contracting during a breastfeeding session.

Use washable underpads at night to absorb any leaks and don't put your favorite sheets on the bed for at least two weeks.

See a doctor if: you're soaking more than one heavy-duty pad an hour, you have a blood clot the size of an egg or larger, feel disoriented, or have a fever. You should also see a doctor if you're still bleeding heavily after 6 weeks.[7]

Vaginal and Perineum Healing

In case you need a refresh, the perineum is the area between the anus and the vulva, and it goes through a lot during the birth – even the most gentle birth. It's normal for your vagina to feel swollen, stretched out, and not quite right after birth. There also may be stinging from any tears or stitches.

Your perineum is going to take some time to heal, especially if you had a tear, stitches, or an episiotomy. An episiotomy is a surgical cut made between the vaginal opening and the anus.

During the first 24 hours after birth, the best way to reduce pain and speed up the recovery process is ice.[8] However, instead of applying the ice directly to your skin, place a thin cloth or pad in between. You can use an ice pack, frozen peas, frozen condoms, or homemade padsicles (see recipe in Chapter 1).

Jocelyn Goodwin

After 24 hours, switch to heat to help soothe and reduce the pain. Draw up a warm bath and include any of the following liquids, herbs, or tea blends to speed up the healing process:

- Witch hazel
- Lavender
- Chamomile
- Red raspberry leaf
- Comfrey
- Yarrow
- Rosemary
- Aloe Vera

If you don't have access to any of the items above or a premade perineum blend, Epsom salt can work wonders.

However, you might find that you don't have time to soak in a warm bath multiple times a day. In this case, you should consider getting a sitz bath. It's a small tub that soaks just your bottom and fits directly on your toilet seat. Alternatively, you can fill up your bath just enough to cover your bottom. Soaking for 10 minutes, 3 times a day is the best way to help the recovery process.

You will also want to ensure that your perineum stays clean. Toilet paper will be too rough, so every time you use the bathroom, use a peri bottle to squirt warm water on your vagina and anus. Additionally, you can use a peri bottle while urinating to help alleviate any stinging from tears or stitches.

There will be a lot of discomfort for the first few weeks, so it is important to have multiple ways to promote healing and ease soreness. A perineal spray, which is an herbal cooling solution, can help ease tenderness and swelling. You can also purchase numbing spray if nothing else dulls the pain.

The most important thing is to rest as much as you can. The pain is usually at its worst when you're sitting, walking, urinating, or passing a bowel movement. The rest of the time, try to stay in bed or lay on the couch. Avoid crossing your legs or using a donut pillow because both of these can pull the wound apart. Any tears you have will take 4-6 weeks to heal, so remember to not overwork yourself and be patient with your recovery.

See a doctor if: your vaginal pain worsens or you have a fever, since this could be a sign of an infection.[9]

Breast Changes

As soon as you give birth, your breasts start going through a lot of changes! They're finally ready to fulfill their purpose. Unfortunately, there's no instant way to notify your body about how you'll be feeding your baby, so you can expect changes whether you're breastfeeding or not. If you choose to bottle feed, your body will stop making milk after several weeks.

What to Expect as Your Breasts Change

Colostrum is the first stage of milk you produce after birth and it's what your baby will eat before your milk comes in. It is often a thick and yellow fluid, and it's very nutrient-dense, so you don't have much of it. Your body will typically produce this for the first 1-3 days after giving birth, and then it will become thinner as your milk starts to come in. If this is the first time you've heard that your milk doesn't come in right away, don't panic. Your little one will be fine because colostrum is the perfect first food for babies.

Once your milk starts to come in, you can expect your breasts to leak pretty regularly. Leakage can happen when your baby is hungry and crying, when you're emotional, when your breasts are very full, and sometimes, for no apparent reason at all. It's best to plan on your shirt being soaked with milk most of the time. To make yourself more comfortable during those first couple weeks of breastfeeding, purchase some disposable or reusable breast pads to avoid leaking everywhere. Although it happens to the best of us, no one wants to be the mom whose shirt is soaked in breast milk in the middle of the grocery store.

If you're breastfeeding your baby, you'll likely be excited when your milk comes in! It's definitely a big milestone. However, it also comes with engorged breasts, which is much less exciting. Engorgement happens when your breasts are extremely full. They might feel like rocks if they're full enough, and this can be very uncomfortable or even painful.

Engorgement is a temporary situation that happens because your body is trying to figure out how much milk to make. Around 8-12 weeks postpartum, your supply will adjust to how much your baby needs and you'll no longer be engorged. In the meantime, placing a wet frozen diaper against your breasts (over a cloth) can help with any discomfort. Moms have also been placing cabbage leaves against their breasts for centuries to reduce pain and this is backed up by current evidence.[10]

You can also expect your nipples to be sore as your body gets used to feeding your baby, even if your baby has a good latch. If soreness continues or breastfeeding becomes very painful, leading to cracked or bleeding nipples, reach out for help. Nipple cream can help your skin stay moisturized, but don't wait to set an appointment with a lactation consultant if you're having problems. The sooner you get help, the sooner you can heal.

Bowel Movement

The first bowel movement after birth can be a scary thing, and can almost feel like you're giving birth again! With everything downstairs swollen and angry, it's normal to dread your first bowel movement. Don't worry, though; no part of your body is going to fall out when you go to the bathroom. Your first bowel movement might be as much as 3-5 days after giving birth, but it could also happen the same day.

It can be helpful to support your perineum by holding a towel or a frozen pad against it to ease some of the pain or to ease your anxiety. As scary as it might seem, when you're ready, don't hold it in. Doing so will increase your risk of getting hemorrhoids (if you're lucky enough not to have them already!). Hemorrhoids are inflamed and swollen veins in the rectum and anus, and they are incredibly common during pregnancy and after giving birth.[11]

Hemorrhoids do shrink over time, but they can cause pain and bleeding during a bowel movement. After every one, be sure to clean your bottom with your peri bottle and pat dry with toilet paper. It's important to avoid wiping until everything is healed. A sitz bath filled with witch hazel can help ease the pain and size of hemorrhoids, and there are also specific hemorrhoid pads you can buy that come pre-made with witch hazel.

See a doctor if: hemorrhoids don't gradually shrink over time.[12]

Constipation

Like your first bowel movement, the idea of constipation may be scary. However, it is normal due to the stress of birth and sometimes medication.

If you are feeling backed up, here are some ways to get things moving:

- Drink 10-12 cups of water per day
- Increase your magnesium intake
- Perform gentle exercise, such as taking a walk
- Eat high-fiber foods
- Take a stool softener or laxative, if necessary

See a doctor if: you haven't had a bowel movement within a week of giving birth, or if you have constant diarrhea.[13]

C-Section Recovery

C-sections are often viewed as a fairly standard way of giving birth these days, but it's important to remember that you will be recovering from a major abdominal surgery. It can take 4-8 weeks before you're able to resume your normal activities, so go easy on yourself. The most important thing is to rest and move gently while you're recovering. You may find it uncomfortable to cough or laugh, so try holding a pillow over your incision if you know either is coming.

As soon as your doctor clears you, start walking around the house to prevent blood clots, even if you don't feel like moving around.[14] For the first few days after birth, you may need pain medication, and your incision will likely be tender for up to 3 weeks after birth.

To care for your incision:

- Keep it clean and dry
- Avoid soaking it in water for the first 3 weeks
- In the shower, let warm, soapy water run over the incision, but do not scrub it
- Pat it dry with a towel after the shower and give it fresh air after to let it completely dry
- If you don't have time to let it dry, set your hairdryer to cold and dry it out

See a doctor if: you have vaginal bleeding that flows like your period more than 4 days after surgery, or a light flow that lasts for 4 weeks after surgery.[15]

Night Sweats

Another uncomfortable reality of postpartum life is night sweats. About ⅓ of all women will experience night sweats or hot flashes in the first month postpartum. This often involves waking up during the night, soaked in sweat. Thankfully, this normally goes away after the first few days or weeks.

During pregnancy, your body retains a lot of water, and sweating is an effective way of getting rid of it. You may find that it helps to sleep on a towel, so you don't have to keep changing the sheet.

It is also important to drink more water. This may seem counterintuitive, but it helps speed up the process of eliminating excess water.

See a doctor if: you have a fever on top of postpartum sweating.[16]

Weight Loss

One of the common misconceptions about giving birth is that suddenly, you'll look like you did pre-pregnancy. Even if you didn't gain a lot of extra weight during the pregnancy, you will likely still look like you're pregnant for a while! There's nothing wrong with that; your body isn't supposed to bounce back right away.

If you're confused as to why you look pregnant after birth, remember that your uterus still has to shrink, you are still retaining extra water, and your skin has been stretched to make room for your baby. You will lose about 10-15 pounds immediately from the weight of the baby, placenta, and amniotic fluid, but after that, your weight loss will be pretty gradual. For both your physical and emotional well-being, it's important not to focus too much on losing weight quickly. If it took you 9 months to gain it, don't expect to lose it overnight.

For the first 6 weeks after labor, focus on providing your body with nutrient-dense foods. You will feel tired and you'll need extra calories to replenish your energy levels. It is estimated that breastfeeding mothers burn an additional 500 calories per day, so listen to your hunger cues.[17] This is not the time to be focusing on weight loss. There might be days when you are constantly hungry and never completely satisfied. It's essential to focus on getting the proper nutrition, not losing weight.

When you do get dressed and look in the mirror, tell yourself how amazing your body is! It can be hard not to think negatively about how you look or how much weight you have gained, but your body did an incredible job of growing and now nurturing a life. You should be proud!

Exercise

After giving birth, exercise is likely one of the last things on your mind, but there will come a time when you'll start thinking about being active again. The 2 exercises you should try to do during postpartum are Kegels and walking.

Kegels

Most women can start doing Kegels the same day they give birth, and it's helpful to start right away! Kegels help heal your pelvic floor muscles, improve your bladder control, and prevent prolapse. A prolapse is your uterus, urethra, or bowel hanging into the vagina.[18]

Here's how to perform Kegel exercises (note that you should have an empty bladder when you start):

1. Find your pelvic floor muscles; you're looking for the one you would use if you were trying to stop the flow of urine or avoid passing gas. You want to avoid tensing your abdomen, thighs, or buttocks, or holding your breath.
2. Tighten your pelvic floor muscles for 3 seconds, then relax for 3 seconds.
3. Repeat for 10-20 seconds each day.

If you can only tighten these muscles for 1 second in the beginning, that's okay. Gradually work up to a 10-second hold.

Walking

Moving around and doing light exercise during the first week after labor is recommended to avoid blood clots, and walking is an excellent option.[19] Doing 1 lap around your house a few times a day is a good starting point, and you can gradually build up from there. You certainly shouldn't be walking 5 miles a week right after giving birth! When you do have the strength and energy to start taking longer walks, getting outside in fresh air can be helpful for your emotional health as well.

Baby Blues

The baby blues are something many moms experience, and they are nothing to be ashamed of. During the first 2 weeks postpartum, you might feel:

- Emotional or weepy over small things
- Sudden mood shifts
- Overwhelmed or stressed
- Nostalgic about your old life
- Impatient and grumpy
- Disinterested in your baby, and guilty about this

All of these feelings are completely normal. Your production of estrogen and progesterone will suddenly decrease after giving birth, and this causes mood swings. 80% of new moms experience this, so you're certainly not alone. Day 3 is often when the baby blues kick in, because you are overwhelmed and exhausted.

Do your best to be kind to yourself during this time, and never underestimate the power of letting some fresh air and sunlight in your house by opening the curtains or windows. Accept that you might feel like nothing is going your way, and that some days, you'll just want to scream or cry! This will pass.

See a doctor if: the emotions last more than 2 weeks or if you have any other concerns about your mental health. If negativity lasts more than 2 weeks, it could be a sign of postpartum depression.[20]

Timeline

Every mom is different, and there are many factors that can impact what the postpartum period looks like, but here's a general timeline of what to expect:

First Week

- You'll have vaginal bleeding (relatively heavy)
- Your uterus will begin to contract
- You'll have your first bowel movement
- You'll experience night sweats
- Your vagina and perineum may hurt a lot, depending on how much was torn
- Your c-section incision will be painful and it might feel difficult to move
- You will likely still look pregnant
- You'll be emotional, with big hormonal swings

- You may feel overwhelmed
- Baby blues might kick in

Second Week

- Your vaginal bleeding will reduce - it's normal for bleeding to last up to and taper out during this second week. The color will change from pinkish-brown to yellowish
- You'll experience less pain and stinging in the perineum area
- You'll have sore nipples and swollen breasts
- You may have clogged ducts
- Any vaginal tear or episiotomy might start itching as it heals
- Your c-section will be tender, but not as painful and uncomfortable. It may start to itch
- You might feel up for a walk around the block

3-5 Weeks

- Your bleeding should dramatically reduce - you may experience some bleeding and discharge (consistently or on and off) for up to 4-6 weeks postpartum
- You'll start to feel more like yourself
- Fatigue will really kick in; you'll feel exhausted and overwhelmed
- You might not be ready for sex, but your vagina should feel more normal
- You'll feel ready to start some light postpartum exercises
- You might still look a little pregnant as your uterus continues to shrink

- You'll really start to connect and bond with your newborn during this period, especially if you didn't feel an intense attachment immediately
- If you had a c-section, you will likely be cleared to drive and lift heavier objects than your baby
- You should look out for signs of postpartum depression and talk to your doctor if you are having intense feelings of depression, hopelessness, or anxiety

6 Weeks

- Your uterus should be back to pre-pregnancy size
- Your vaginal bleeding will likely stop
- You will probably be cleared for sexual activity and moderate exercise
- A c-section scar might be very itchy or numb
- You will continue to feel exhausted and overwhelmed, but hopefully slightly more positive
- You may be cleared to resume normal life, although you may not yet feel up to it

6 weeks-6 months

- You may start to notice these symptoms (if you haven't already): postpartum hair loss, low bladder control, hot flashes, low libido, vaginal dryness, pelvic floor dysfunction
- Your period may return, depending on whether you're breastfeeding or not and how frequently
- You can return to regular sexual activity
- Your muscle tone and connective tissue will be restored

3
First Week With Your Baby

No matter how much you prepare for the first week with your newborn, you're going to be dealing with a lot of emotions. Not knowing what normal newborn behavior looks like can lead to significantly more anxiety, so this chapter will help you understand what to expect.

Reality

No amount of classes or books can prepare you for the surge of emotions you feel when they place your newborn on your chest for the first time. Most people are overwhelmed by love and joy in those first few moments... but it's not long before reality sets in and you start to wonder – am I really prepared for this?

Taking care of a baby is a skill that has to be learned, and that's a good thing. Each individual will work out their own way of approaching this. With every passing day, you'll feel a little more comfortable. It's okay to be new at this. We were all there at one point!

For most moms, the first 6 weeks are the most challenging. Expect them to be intense. You'll feed your newborn around the clock and they will most likely cry anytime you put them down. On top of that, you'll be incredibly sleep-deprived and have very little energy or time to tend to your own needs.

If you're imagining the first few days passing with your newborn sleeping soundly in a crib, know this isn't the reality for most. Newborns do sleep a lot, but they're also used to being inside your womb and will likely want to be near you or held by you most of the time. When it all feels overwhelming, try to take it one day at a time.

When you start to feel like you don't recognize yourself anymore, give yourself a break. Your whole life has just changed and no one has it all figured out right away. Instead of trying to get your baby on a schedule immediately, focus on what you can control, like taking care of your own physical and mental health. Remember, don't compare your reality to anyone else's highlight reel. You're doing a great job!

Before You Leave the Hospital

After the birth of your newborn, the panic might set in when you realize you have to leave the hospital. Now don't get me wrong; the comfort of your own home is preferable to the hospital, but at the hospital, you're not on your own. You might find yourself wondering, are they really going to let me take my baby home? It feels like you should need to get a license or pass a test first.

Most moms will spend 1 or 2 nights in the hospital. Before you leave, they will do a basic check-up for your baby, which will include:

- Taking their temperature
- Measuring their weight, length, and head circumference

- APGAR test, which is done at 1 and 5 minutes after birth to test many of their vital signs
- Vitamin K shot
- Hearing test
- Antibiotic eye drops or ointment
- Jaundice test
- Newborn screening
- Hepatitis B vaccine

That may seem like a lot of tests, but they are all there to ensure your baby is healthy and thriving outside your womb. Rest assured that they won't send you home until it's safe for you and your baby to go.

Before you're discharged from the hospital, make sure you ask for any help you need. If you feel you need support with how to hold, burp, change, or care for your newborn, ask a nurse or your midwife. You're not an inconvenience or a burden; they're specifically there to help you and will be glad to answer any questions you have. Remember, this is their job and they deal with questions like this all the time.

If you're planning on breastfeeding, make sure you get guidance on this. Your hospital should have a lactation specialist, who will be able to ensure your newborn is latching correctly.

It's a good idea to ask for recommendations on the best lactation consultants, postpartum doulas, or newborn nurses so you know who to contact if their services are needed. You can also ask what kind of over-the-counter medicine you can take for any pain or other issues.

Going Home

Now the real adventure begins! It's normal for panic to set in at this point. Most first-time parents feel unsure. All of a sudden, you're on your own, trying to remember everything you've read about how to care for your baby.

Take a deep breath and trust your instincts. You have them for a reason, and they'll often be your greatest guide.

Newborns may seem fragile, but try not to be afraid of handling your little one. It can be helpful to pay attention to the way your nurse handles your baby in the hospital, but as long as you're gentle, you're not going to break them!

While you're trying to remember all the important stuff, here are several rules of thumb to remember when holding your baby:

- Wash your hands (and have everyone else wash their hands!) before handling your newborn
- Always support the baby's head and neck when you're holding them
- Avoid shaking your newborn, even while playing. This means avoiding bouncing them on your knee or throwing them in the air

For the car ride home, you should have the car seat ready to go when your partner arrives at the hospital. Follow the manual for guidance on installing your individual car seat. Every car seat is different, but in general, you shouldn't be able to move the car seat if you push on it, and the chest clips should be level with your baby's armpits. Your newborn should be buckled in securely enough that they don't bounce or move around while the car is in motion.

Once you get home, try to get some rest to prepare for your first week with your new baby.

First Week

The first week can be a flurry of emotions, both positive and negative, and the sheer newness of the experience can be overwhelming. Your newborn's behavior will change a lot over the first few days. Every baby is different, but there are some commonalities between them, unless you have a "unicorn baby" that feeds every 4 hours and sleeps throughout the night. Unfortunately, this isn't likely to be the case. With that in mind, let's look at what each day will look like with your newborn.

Day 1

For the first 24 hours, you'll likely still be in the hospital, but expect those hours to be mostly full of bliss! Enjoy that after-birth high. That new baby smell. If only things could stay like this! Cherish these moments while they last.

Your baby will be relatively settled and calm because they've been through a lot, just like you. They might not cry much at first and will likely sleep a lot, especially right after birth. Don't get too used to this behavior, though.

It's not always easy, but – especially if you have support from your partner – try to rest during this time.

Lots of cuddling and skin-to-skin should happen during the first day. Skin-to-skin means your newborn is laid directly on your bare chest, and this offers many benefits for both you and your baby.

Skin-to-skin contact will help:

- Regulate the baby's heart rate and breathing
- Regulate the baby's temperature
- Allow friendly bacteria to pass from the mother to the baby, protecting them from infections

- Adjust your baby to life outside the womb
- Encourage breastfeeding
- Stimulate the digestion
- Allow you to develop a close, loving relationship with your baby[1]

Skin-to-skin is not just for the mom; plenty of contact between your baby and your partner can have many of these benefits as well.

If your baby was born by c-section or you had a quick vaginal birth, expect your baby to be pretty mucusy. It can take up to 48 hours for all of the mucus to be cleared out of their system, and it's normal for them to gag, vomit, sneeze, or poop mucus. It's also possible that they won't be very interested in feeding at first due to the excess mucus in their stomach.[2]

If you had a birth where forceps or a vacuum were required, your newborn may be more irritable due to a slightly swollen or sore head. If they have a bruise on the back of their head, it may be uncomfortable for them to lie in a crib. Instead, try having them lie with their chest against your chest until this heals.

After birth, it can take 40 minutes or longer for your newborn to get to the breast. Newborns instinctively search for the breast, so you might notice them bobbing their head around, looking for it.[3]

If you're planning to bottle-feed, you do not need to bring any feeding supplies to the hospital, as most hospitals won't allow you to use your own bottle or formula. Instead, they will provide you with premixed formula in ready-to-go bottles. During the first week, your baby should only be drinking 1 to 2 ounces of infant formula every 2 to 3 hours.[4]

It's normal for a healthy baby to only have 2 good feeds in the first 12 hours. Ideally, your newborn should feed within 2 hours of their birth and again within 12 hours. In the first 24 hours especially, it's okay to wake your baby to feed them, since they're incredibly sleepy during this time.[5] Both you and your baby will be getting the hang of feeding and it's okay to feel completely overwhelmed at first.

Wondering if your newborn is getting enough nutrients is a normal concern for new moms. When you're breastfeeding, you don't actually see how much your baby is consuming. The stomach of a newborn is relatively tiny, and it doesn't take much to fill them up, so the best way to tell if your baby is eating enough is how many diapers they're wetting.

Your newborn should have 1-2 wet diapers or more per day during the first 2 days.[6] If you still feel unsure of whether your baby is eating enough, it may ease your mind to hand express a small amount of colostrum, just to be sure something is coming out. Also, keep in mind that it's normal for babies to lose weight after birth, and most babies will return to at least their birth weight within 2 weeks.

When it comes to dirty diapers, your baby should also have at least 1 poop within the first 24 hours of birth. Their first poop is called meconium, and is black or dark green, sticky like tar, and odorless.[7] It can be hard to clean off their bum because it's so sticky, so using some olive oil on the skin can be effective.

Many new moms spend a lot of time watching their newborns to make sure they're breathing, especially in those first few days. It's normal for newborns to breathe quickly, pause for a few seconds, and then start breathing again. It's also common for newborns to sound congested, since mucus can build up quickly in their tiny nasal passages.

See a doctor if: your baby is grunting, flaring their nostrils, breathing rapidly for long periods, wheezing from the chest, pausing for more than 10-15 seconds between breaths, having chest retractions, or breathing heavily and noisily.

Lastly, be aware that the beautiful, smooth baby skin that we're used to doesn't always appear during the newborn phase. It's normal for newborns to have newborn rash, cradle cap, or peeling and dryness from the amniotic fluid.

Here are some common aspects of a newborn's appearance:

- Cone-shaped head due to squeezing in the birth canal
- Blue hands and feet
- Swollen face and eyes
- Multiple birthmarks that may fade over time
- Lanugo, which are fine hairs on your newborn's shoulders, back, and any other place they have hair follicles. These hairs usually fall out after a week or two[8]

Your newborn's hands, feet, and face will also likely feel chilly during the first week after birth. Feel in between their shoulder blades or touch their breastbone to check if they're too cold or too warm.

Day 2

Day 1 may have been overwhelming and also full of bliss, but Day 2 is when the madness begins. It's as if they are making up for being a perfect angel yesterday. Your newborn will become more alert and want to feed more often, typically every 1-3 hours.

Once the sun sets during the late afternoon or evening, your baby may become fussy and unsettled, and might be fighting sleep. They will likely want lots of attention and skin-to-skin time, and may want to nurse more. It is also common for them to want lots of short feeds over a few hours, which feels like a feeding frenzy. When your newborn wants to eat, you may notice them giving you hunger cues such as turning their cheek toward you or "searching for food" with their mouth. These are all signs of healthy development.

Day 2 will culminate in a long night for many new parents, especially with the cycle of putting your baby on the breast and off the breast, putting them down, and then picking them up. It may feel like neither of you gets much sleep. If you feel like something is wrong with your baby by this point, know that you're not alone. It's normal for them to act this way and normal for you to feel this way too.

No matter how frequently you feed your baby, you're not going to overfeed them. It might feel impossible for them to want more after eating 20 minutes ago, but at this point, your breasts are still producing colostrum before your milk comes in. Biologically, colostrum is the perfect first food for your newborn to support their immune system and gut health. Your newborn's stomach is tiny, so they are getting all the nutrients they need, but they may constantly feel hungry and not satisfied because colostrum is produced in lower quantities.

Luckily, babies are born with brown fat and they use this energy during the first few days until your milk comes in. This is what leads to newborns losing 7-10% of their birth weight by Day 5, but gaining most of that weight back in the first 2 weeks after birth.[9]

The good news is, your baby knows biologically that feeding frequently over a short period of time is what encourages your body to produce more milk. Milk production is based on supply and demand, so the more they feed, the more milk your body will produce, and the quicker your milk will come in.

You might wonder why they don't feed like this during the day instead of the night. The answer is that babies like to feed at night because the levels of prolactin, the hormone that makes your milk, are highest at night.[10]

This behavior of wanting to feed constantly in the later afternoon and night is mostly seen in breastfed babies because they are priming their mothers to produce milk. Formula-fed babies usually feed less frequently than breastfed ones because formula takes longer to digest.

If you have a baby girl, they may experience something called false menstruation. This means they may bleed from their vagina. This can happen anywhere from Day 2 up until Day 10, but it normally only lasts for 3-4 days. This false menstruation doesn't happen to all baby girls, but they might have some bloody mucus in their vagina, which could be pinkish or bright red. Babies are exposed to a number of hormones in the womb, but after birth, these hormone levels start to drop and can cause vaginal bleeding. Once the bleeding has gone, it shouldn't return.[11]

You might also notice your baby has newborn breasts for the first couple of days, and this can happen to both male and female babies. They might have breast buds with firm lumps under the nipples, or swollen breasts. They might even leak a few drops of milk out of their nipples.[12] These are all very normal things.

Days 3 & 4

According to the American Academy of Pediatrics (AAP), babies should get their first checkup 3-5 days after birth.[13] So if you haven't already, be sure you get your newborn scheduled for an appointment.

It is likely that your baby will sleep best in the early hours of the morning, so use this time to take a nap or a shower, or just do something for yourself. Rest and self-care are essential during the first week in particular. The night on Day 3 will likely be similar to the previous night. Typically, nights 2 and 3 are the hardest and you may start to wonder if you can really do this. The answer is yes, you can! Remember, no night lasts forever, no matter how long it is.

Your baby's stomach grows from the size of a large marble to the size of a ping-pong ball at this stage.[14] Your body will start increasing its milk supply as it transitions from colostrum to milk, and your baby will continue to be constantly on the breast to encourage your body to make enough milk to fill their growing tummy.

By Days 3 and 4, you might notice your milk coming in. This is something to celebrate, even if you don't feel like celebrating at the moment. When your milk comes in, your breasts may feel tingly, warm, and firm, and if you have smaller breasts, it may feel more intense. There are some factors that can delay your milk coming in, such as birth by c-section, hormonal issues, thyroid conditions, gestational diabetes, PCOS, or heavy bleeding after birth.

Even though you have a higher volume of milk now, your baby will eat more than you think. Expect them to feed every 2-4 hours as they catch up on calories.

You'll also start to notice diaper changes increase. By this point, your baby should have 3 or more pee-filled diapers each day, and the diapers should be fuller than they were previously.[15] Your baby may poop 2 or more times a day. As your milk starts to come in, you'll notice your baby's stool change to a greenish color. It should be thinner and less sticky than meconium.

During the day, your newborn will likely be calm and easy to settle. There may also be a larger gap between feedings during the day. At night, continue to expect more frequent feedings and little sleep for you and your partner. It's also normal for your baby to nap during the day in their crib or bassinet, but want to sleep in your arms at night. Sleep safety is crucial, especially during the newborn phase.

Although co-sleeping isn't recommended by the AAP and most parents swear they'll never do it beforehand, many parents who end up co-sleeping didn't plan on it. You might do it by accident, or you might find it works well for your family, but it's important to have a game plan for when your baby won't sleep in their crib or bassinet. A recent study by the CDC showed that more than half of parents co-sleep at some point, so it is important to know how to do it safely.[16]

In Chapter 6, we'll go over safe ways to co-sleep or bed share with your baby.

Another option that some parents will turn to is having one parent hold the baby while the other one sleeps. If you choose to do this at night, the parent watching the baby shouldn't sit on the sofa or an armchair with the baby, since these are not safe places to co-sleep. There's too much risk of accidentally nodding off. This parent should stand and hold the baby, or sit on a yoga ball instead.

It is also important to note that if you choose for your partner to introduce a bottle during the night so you can get some sleep, this can negatively affect your milk supply.

Days 5, 6, & 7

By Day 5, your milk should be fully in. Your newborn will continue to be calm during the day and more alert at night, and they should start to gain weight back since they're getting more milk.

At this point, your newborn should have a wet diaper for every feed, so 5 or more a day.[17] This is a good indicator that they are getting enough milk. They should also have 2 poops a day by Day 5. For breastfed babies, their stools will likely be mustard colored. It's normal for them to be runny, almost like diarrhea. You may notice what looks like seeds in your baby's dirty diaper, which are actually congealed milk or milk curds. Pay attention to what your baby's poop looks like and check for consistency from day to day.

If your baby is formula fed, their poop may be yellow or brown, with a thicker consistency, like peanut butter. It's common for them to have fewer stools than breastfed babies, but they are normally bigger and smellier.

Over the next few weeks, a formula-fed baby will gradually consume more during each feed, till they take around 3 to 4 ounces per feed.[18] The amount and frequency of feeds should always be adjusted based on your baby's hunger cues.

See a doctor if: there is whitish mucus or flecks of red in your baby's stool.[19]

Falling in Love With Your Baby

Most stories of what happens after birth show moms immediately falling in love with their babies, and the rush of oxytocin after birth does help with that! However, this doesn't happen for every mom. If you feel like you don't have a connection with your newborn right away, or didn't feel the overwhelming love everyone else seems to experience, this doesn't mean you're a bad mom. For some, building that connection takes time. And that's okay!

Can You Spoil Your Week-old Newborn?

Speaking of building a connection with your baby, if you receive any unsolicited advice during this period, there's a good chance you'll hear something about spoiling your baby. So, can you spoil your newborn baby? The short answer is no. You're not going to spoil your baby by holding them too much, no matter what anyone else says.

When you think about it, your baby just spent 9 months inside you. During that time, they were constantly warm and able to hear your heartbeat 24/7. This is the first time they have ever been separated from you. Can you really blame them for wanting to only sleep in your arms, or for crying any time they're away from you?

This doesn't make it any easier to deal with, but know that it's normal for your baby to respond this way. To your baby, you are warmth, comfort, food, and safety. They feel vulnerable if they're not around you.

Not only is it impossible for you to create a bad habit of holding them too much at this stage, but studies show that high levels of dependence in the early years lead to greater independence later on.[20] The more they feel they can rely on you as a safety net, the more likely they are to feel confident trying things on their own. You are teaching them that if they fall, you will be there to pick them up.

All the same, it can be exhausting to feel like you never get a break from holding your baby. When you feel you need one, be honest with your partner, a family member, or a friend about it. It's totally okay to get someone else to hold the little one so you can take a nap or a shower uninterrupted.

Environment

Bringing your newborn home is a new experience for you, but remember that everything, including the environment at home, is a new experience for your baby. Keep in mind that babies are sensitive to light, touch, and sound.

Try dim lighting to keep your baby comfortable and calm, especially at night. It might be beneficial to get a red night light that gives you enough light to see your baby during diaper changes and latching, but is not bright enough to be uncomfortable for you or your baby.

Babies are also only used to muffled sounds after being in your womb for 9 months. Try to avoid loud noises and use a white noise machine to mimic the sounds they heard in the womb.

5 Senses

Newborns experience their 5 senses differently than older children do. Here's how your newborn baby experiences each of their senses.

Sight: Newborn babies only see in black and white, with shades of gray, right after birth. They will start to develop color vision as time goes on. They can also see only 8-10 inches in front of them.[21]

Touch: Newborns are always comforted by touch, and infant massages, as well as skin-to-skin contact, are great for calming them down. Remember, you can't spoil a newborn, so hold them as much as they want to be held. Use a baby carrier when they want to be held for long periods and you need to get something done.

Smell: Studies have shown that newborns have a strong sense of smell. Since mom is the one they're used to, newborns love the smell of their mothers, especially their breast milk.[22]

Hearing: Newborns typically prefer high-pitched voices over deep voices. It's important to stimulate their hearing by talking, singing, reading out loud, playing light music, or reciting nursery rhymes. They can also recognize voices that they heard from the womb.

Taste: Newborns prefer sweet tastes over sour or bitter tastes, and have a strong preference for breast milk.[23]

Bathing

Until your newborn's umbilical stump falls off, typically between 1-4 weeks, only give them sponge baths. If your baby is circumcised, only do sponge baths until it's fully healed, which should be 1-2 weeks after surgery.[24]

Here's how to give a sponge bath:

1. Start with a warm room. Use a flat surface, like a table or counter covered with a towel, or a sink without water in it.
2. Fill a nearby sink or bowl with warm water. The temperature should be around 100°F or 38°C. Check it with your elbow or wrist to ensure it's not too hot.
3. First, use water only to wipe their eyes, from the inner corner to the outer corner. Cotton balls can be great for this. Then, wipe their nose and ears with a different part of a washcloth or a new cotton ball. Wash their face last.
4. Use water and soap to clean their scalp and the rest of their body. Focus on under their arms, behind their ears, and around the neck and genital area.
5. Make sure all areas, including all the cracks and crevices, are dry before diapering and clothing them.

If you're in a hurry, you can occasionally wipe them down with unscented wipes instead of doing a sponge bath. When using wipes, focus just on their neck folds, under their arms, and their genitals.

Clothes

When you're pregnant, it's fun to buy the cutest outfits for your baby. There's nothing wrong with splurging on some lovely things for your baby to wear, but during the first few weeks, focus on what's comfortable and easy to put on. Some great clothes are:

- One-piece bodysuits
- Footed pajamas
- Swaddles
- A sleep sack for colder nights

If your newborn dislikes having clothes pulled over their head or their umbilical cord stump is sensitive, you can put them in one-piece outfits that snap at the side, often called side snap kimonos. No matter what outfit you put them in, always make sure their clothes and diapers aren't too tight or too loose.

The hospital will likely put a hat on your newborn right away to help regulate their temperature. However, once your baby is ready to go home, they should be able to regulate their temperature without hats and mittens. It is also advised by the AAP to never put your baby to sleep wearing a hat.[25]

Visitors

Your family and friends will want to visit you and your new baby when you come home from the hospital, but remember that it's up to you to decide when you feel comfortable having visitors.

Once you do, don't be afraid to put time restrictions on their visits. You can also decide beforehand whether you'll allow visitors to hold your baby. It's okay if you choose not to! Even if someone else is upset about this, stand your ground. If that's likely to be a challenge for you, try setting boundaries ahead of time so your visitors know what to expect.

Don't be afraid to ask for help. It doesn't make you selfish to ask your visitors to contribute in some way. You might ask each visitor to do one thing for you, and here are some examples:

- Unload the dishwasher
- Fold a load of laundry
- Hold your baby so you can shower
- Bring you a meal
- Make you a cup of tea
- Walk the dog

Many people aren't sure what to do when they visit a new mom, and asking them for help makes them feel useful. We also have a tendency, especially as moms, to feel like we have to do it all. Asking for help doesn't make you weak.

You should expect your family and friends to have opinions about certain things when they visit. This might make you feel anxious or even insecure as a new mom, like they think you don't know what to do or have what it takes. You certainly don't have to accept their advice, but try to be open to it. It's okay to be new at something, and you might also be surprised what wisdom they can offer you from their own experience.

4

Secrets to Successful Breastfeeding

No matter how you spin it, breastfeeding is challenging for most women. You might think, breastfeeding is natural, so shouldn't it come naturally? This isn't necessarily the case, and there's generally a learning curve. When you get the hang of it, breastfeeding can be an incredible bonding experience between you and your baby, but there's a lack of acknowledgment for how difficult breastfeeding can be in the beginning.

Like many other aspects of motherhood, breastfeeding is a skill that takes time to learn. During the first few days and weeks, you will feel an intense need to feed your baby. It's likely going to be a struggle at first, as you spend the early days wondering whether your baby is eating enough, dealing with regulating your milk supply, and addressing any potential latch issues.

With the right help and support, breastfeeding does get easier with time and can become the easiest way to feed your baby. It doesn't require any preparation or equipment and you can leave the house with your little one without having to worry about how much formula you need, or cleaning and sterilizing bottles.

So, if breastfeeding is so challenging for most women, why are so many new moms surprised when they struggle to breastfeed? And why do so many new moms stop breastfeeding instead of getting the help they need? Both of these things can be attributed to a lack of knowledge. In the past, breastfeeding support and guidance would be passed down from generation to generation, but in our modern world, many young mothers have never been exposed to breastfeeding, let alone taught how to do it.

In Western culture, formula became pretty popular in the 1950s. At the time, the dominant attitude was that breastfeeding was something practiced by uneducated mothers and the lower classes. It was considered old-fashioned and even "disgusting," seen as something only women who couldn't afford formula would do. Why would women need to breastfeed when they could just buy formula?

Breastfeeding didn't regain popularity until the 1970s, and by 2013, 4 out of 5 infants started out breastfeeding. Although this represents a huge shift in the attitude toward breastfeeding, only about half of those same babies were still breastfeeding by 6 months old.[1]

Despite the challenges of breastfeeding, it's possible to have a successful breastfeeding relationship with your baby. Knowing when to get help is a significant part of breastfeeding success.

Breastfeeding Basics

Good breastfeeding starts with recognizing hunger cues. An overly hungry baby will also be fussier and harder to calm down. Particularly during the newborn phase, trying to get your baby to latch during a feed can feel like a lot of work, so it's best to offer a feed before your baby gets too hungry. In Chapter 7, we will discuss hunger cues in more detail. It's also important to remember that breastfeeding is a two-way relationship and if your breasts are uncomfortably full, you can offer food to your baby even if they aren't showing hunger cues.

At the start of each breastfeeding session, you should be:

- Relaxed: babies can sense how you feel. Take a few deep breaths, drop your shoulders, and uncurl your toes. Find something that will help you relax if necessary, such as playing calming music.
- Comfortable: you will be in this position for 15-45 minutes, so you want to ensure you're supported. If you have a breastfeeding pillow or another support pillow, have it in the proper position or close by so you can prop up your arms. Find a stool for your feet if they're not touching the ground.

Each mom and baby's breastfeeding journey will be unique, since all of our bodies and babies are different. However, here are the basics on how to get a good position and latch.

Positioning

The laid back, or reclined position, can be a great first position to try. Typically, mothers have less nipple pain and trauma in this position because it triggers their baby's natural feeding reflexes, which leads to an effortless and deeper latch.[2]

To get in this position, support yourself at a 45-degree angle with both of your arms propped on pillows. Your baby should have their full weight on your body, with their feet pressing against your thighs, tummy, or a pillow. Use one hand to support your baby's neck and the other to support your breast, if needed. Your baby can be diagonal across your body, straight, or sideways (for c-section moms.) If they are sideways, remember to place a pillow under their feet for support.

Latching On

Once you and your baby are in the proper position, it's time to latch on. The goal is to get a deep latch so that your nipple is toward the back of their mouth, where their soft palate is. Nipple trauma is often caused by the nipple rubbing against the hard palate in the middle of the mouth due to a shallow latch.

The steps to getting a deep latch are:

1. Hold your baby close, with their nose touching your nipple and their chin touching your breast. Be careful not to start with their mouth against your nipple. Starting too high can lead to a shallow latch.
2. Mouth opens - once your baby smells your nipple, they will start searching for it, tilting their head back and

opening their mouth. Their top lip will then line up with your nipple. If they don't open their mouth right away, you can gently tickle their nose and upper lip with your nipple or even hand express a drop of milk to get them interested.

3. Bring the baby toward the breast - once their mouth is wide open, quickly bring the baby to your breast, chin first. It's important to bring them in quickly with a little bit of force to help them get a mouthful of your breast. Don't worry, your breast isn't going to hurt your baby! Always bring your baby to your breast, not the other way around, to avoid being hunched over. At this point, they should have both the nipple and areola in their mouth and your nipple should be at the roof of your baby's mouth. You should be able to see more areola above your baby's top lip than their bottom lip, depending on the size of your areola. Their chin should be buried deep in the breast and their nose should be clear, since their head is tilted back. This position allows their tongue to touch as much breast as possible.

. . .

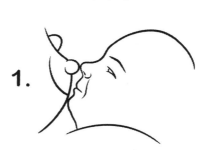

1.

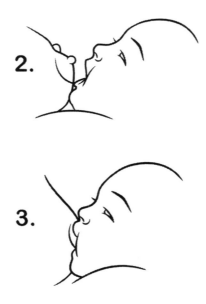

At this point, your baby's tongue will pull your nipple toward the back of their mouth. The nipple will get sucked to 2-3 times its original length and reach the soft palate in the back of the mouth. It's normal to have 30-40 seconds of toe-curling pain that suddenly stops.

If the baby's latch was successful, their lips should be full, rounded, and turned outward as they feed, almost like a fish! They should also be sucking rhythmically and deeply in short bursts separated by pauses.

Helpful Tips

- If their lips are not flared out like a fish, use your thumb to gently push down on your baby's chin to widen their latch and push out their bottom lip.
- Use a foot support for your baby. It's important to have their feet pressing against your thighs, tummy, or a pillow

instead of dangling. This support helps keep their mouth completely open and lets them get a deep latch.[3]

- Support their upper back and neck during the feeding, instead of the back of their head. Keep the top of your fingers at the base of their skull. Always avoid putting your hand on the back of their head during nursing. This makes it difficult for babies to relax due to being restricted and feeling like they won't be able to unlatch when they want to.

- Support your breast before latching and during feeding by using a C shape or a U shape. You can make a C shape by cupping your breast from the side or a U shape by using your entire hand to lift your breast from underneath. Be sure to hold your breast at the base so there's plenty of room for your baby to latch without your hand being in the way.

C shape   **U shape**

- Avoid putting a hat on your baby during feedings. Research shows that hats can decrease their feeding instincts. As long as you're warm and they have a blanket or clothes on, their temperature will be stable and they don't need to wear a hat.[4]

- If your baby is fussing by pulling at your breast with their gums, coming off the breast, or squirming around, they most likely need to be burped or are ready to move to the other breast. In some instances, your milk might be coming down too quickly or forcefully, and they're having trouble swallowing.

Ending the Nursing Session

Especially in the early days, you might be afraid your baby isn't getting enough milk, so how can you tell when your baby has finished nursing? When you're breastfeeding, there isn't a specific amount of time that your baby needs to feed. Allow your baby to suck at your breast for as long as they like and offer the second breast if they want it. If you let them decide how long to feed for, they'll get all the nutrients they need.

Some babies will always nurse from both breasts, some will occasionally nurse from both, and some will never go on to the second breast in one session. If your baby only nurses from one side, just switch to the opposite side next feeding. If you can't remember which breast you left off on, just check which breast feels fuller.

Once your baby has finished nursing, examine your nipple. It's a good indicator of a healthy latch if it's the same shape as it was before but longer. If your nipple is flattened or slanted like a new tube of lipstick, or it's white like your baby has been cutting off the blood supply, this indicates a shallow latch. You can also feel your breast after nursing. If your breast is uniformly soft, this is a great indicator that your baby had a good feed.

There's a lot of emphasis on burping babies after a feed, but not all babies will need to burp. It's best to try burping your baby in the beginning until you know whether they need it or not. It may also be helpful to offer a burp before switching to the second breast. Overall, don't stress too much about it. We will cover burping methods in more depth in Chapter 7.

Other Breastfeeding Positions

Cradle Hold

The cradle hold is a classic position and is what most of us picture when we think of breastfeeding. However, statistically, it causes the most nipple pain.[5] In this position, you are sitting upright, with your baby on their side, with their head and neck resting on your forearm. Their stomach should be touching your stomach.

Rugby/Football Hold

This position is good for nursing twins, for women with larger breasts, for moms who have had a c-section, or for moms with flat or inverted nipples. It gives you a good view of the baby's mouth and your nipple. For the rugby/football hold, your baby's body should be under your armpit and their butt should be behind you, in the same way you would hold a football. It may be helpful to have a pillow under your elbow that's supporting your baby.

Side-Lying Position

The side-lying position is great for when you're tired and is a natural choice for night-time feedings. It can also be great for moms who have had a c-section. However, it's not always the best position for a newborn, since your baby isn't as supported in this position. For this position, you and your baby lie on your sides, facing one another, belly to belly.

Upright Breastfeeding or Koala Hold

Your baby will be sitting upright, facing you, and straddling your knee. This is a good position for babies who suffer from reflux or ear infections. It's also good for babies with a tongue-tie or low muscle tone, and it's often a position that older babies will use.

If you're breastfeeding in any position other than a reclined position (where your baby's weight is on you), be sure to get close and press your baby's body tightly against yours. Also, make sure their head is always straight, not turning to the side, regardless of the position.

Nipple Variations

Women's nipples come in all shapes and sizes, but this can impact the breastfeeding experience.

In general, there are 4 different categories that nipples fall into:

- Protruding nipples that are always erect

- Typical nipples that are flat until you touch, stimulate, or chill them; then they become erect
- Flat nipples that stay the same even when you stimulate them
- Inverted nipples that are retracted into the breast, usually appearing like a slit across the breast, with the nipple inside. They may protrude when they are stimulated or cold, or they may stay inverted

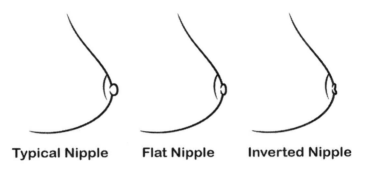

Typical Nipple   **Flat Nipple**   **Inverted Nipple**

You might have nipples of two different types as well, such as one inverted and one protruding nipple. All nipples perform differently, but you may have to make some adjustments while breastfeeding, depending on the type you have.

For protruding and typical nipples, there's no special preparation needed.

For flat and inverted nipples, keep in mind that it's breastfeeding, not nipple feeding, so in most cases, once your baby starts sucking, your nipple will come out. If not, it is important to use one of the following techniques prior to nursing:

- Roll your nipple between your thumb and forefinger to encourage it to stick out

- Touch your nipple briefly with a cold compress or ice cube
- Hand express, or use a breast pump or nipple corrector for a couple of minutes before each feeding session
- Use the Hoffman technique, which involves placing your thumbs at the right and left edges of the areola. While putting slight pressure on the base of the nipple, pull your thumbs firmly apart. Rotate your thumbs around the areola so they're at the top and bottom. Repeat this technique for a minute or so each day and you may see the nipple progressively start to stick out.

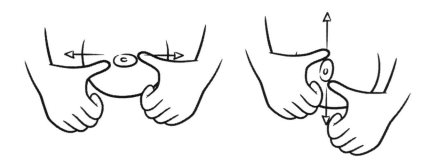

Breast Variations

Like nipples, breasts also come in all shapes and sizes. The glandular tissue in the breast is made up of the cells that produce milk. All women have the same number of cells, regardless of breast size. Fat makes breasts different sizes, but it doesn't impact how much milk you have. Regardless of the size of your breasts, you can successfully breastfeed your baby!

If you do have large breasts, it may take some time for you to find your groove while feeding your baby. It can be challenging to position and hold your baby, and you want to ensure you're not blocking your baby's nose while feeding.

The rugby or football hold can be effective for women with larger breasts. It may also be helpful to hold your breasts in C or U shape while feeding, depending on the position. You might also use a rolled-up towel and place it under your breast to lift your nipple.

Helpful Aids for Breastfeeding

In theory, all you need to breastfeed your baby is a breast and your baby! That said, moms who have breastfed know it's not always as simple as that. Here are some aids to help you during your breastfeeding journey.

Hand Expressing

Hand expressing can be a great way to build your confidence in the beginning. It is also an essential skill for relieving pressure in your breasts when you are engorged, and it doesn't require any equipment.

Engorgement happens to many new moms when their milk first comes in. Even though they want milk, babies don't typically love nursing from a full, hard breast. If you release a bit of the milk, it will make it easier for them to latch on and successfully nurse. If you hand expressed pre-birth, you will be happy to know that expressing milk is a lot easier than colostrum.

To hand express:

1. Warm the breast by pressing a warm washcloth against your breast or taking a warm shower.
2. Sit up straight so you are working with gravity.
3. Massage the breast lightly with your hands and fingertips to stimulate your milk ejection reflex. This can be done by placing a flat hand on the top and bottom of the breast and move your hands in a circular motion.

4. Cup your pointer finger and thumb in a C on your "sweet spot." This could be anywhere from on the edge of your areola to an inch away from your areola. Experiment with different distances. Your thumb and pointer finger should be in a straight line with your nipple.

5. Pull your thumb and pointer finger back into the breast, gently squeeze, and relax. Repeat in a rhythmic movement. Don't expect to see any milk/colostrum come out of the breast in the beginning. It may take a few minutes, so be patient.

6. Gradually, your breast milk/colostrum will start to drip out. You are looking for a small spray of milk as opposed to a dribble.

7. Rotate your hand around the areola every few compressions or whenever the milk flow stops.

8. Alternate back and forth between the breasts or do each breast separately.

Breast Compressions

Breast compression is a way to release more milk, but it's done toward the end of a feeding session instead of at the beginning.

Breast compression is simply a long, gentle squeeze of the breast to encourage proper milk flow.

To do a breast compression:

1. Wait until your baby stops actively sucking but is still latched. It should feel as if they're taking a pause
2. Squeeze down with your thumb on the top of your breast and with your finger on the bottom. Continue to hold the breast compression until your baby stops sucking, and then release
3. Rotate your hand around the breast and repeat.

Breast compressions are great to do before your baby switches to the other breast, when the thick, fattier milk has come down and your baby is tired

Nipple Shields

A nipple shield is an artificial silicone nipple that covers your nipple to help feed your baby if you're struggling with breastfeeding. The silicone nipple is longer and firmer than a real nipple, which helps infants who have trouble latching. This nipple easily hits the back of your baby's mouth, triggering the sucking reflex.

Although they have a lot of benefits, nipple shields are almost a dirty word in the breastfeeding community and can be highly controversial. You should examine the pros and cons to determine what's best for you and your baby.

Pros:

- They can save a breastfeeding relationship when you're about to give up, or they can help you get your breastfeeding journey off to a good start

- They can be helpful for premature babies, babies with tongue-ties, babies who are used to a bottle, women with inverted or flat nipples, or nipple trauma that makes it difficult to breastfeed
- Normally, your baby can be transitioned off of them, so you don't have to use them forever

Cons:

- Many people use them as a way to fix an issue instead of looking for the cause, and this means you'll have to depend on the shield permanently
- It's harder to get a deep latch and your baby might not stimulate the breast fully. They won't get enough milk, which could lead to you not producing enough milk or suffering from mastitis or a clogged duct
- For some women, it can cause more pain, especially if they use the wrong size shield

Overall, a nipple shield can help in a lot of situations, but you should also contact a lactation consultant or breastfeeding specialist for help solving the actual issue. Using a nipple shield isn't ideal, but if they help you have a successful breastfeeding journey, don't stress about using them.

A Good Breastfeeding Pillow

A good nursing or breastfeeding pillow isn't necessary, but it can make your breastfeeding journey much more comfortable. If you don't have one or aren't sure if you need one, regular pillows can often work as well.

When you are using a breastfeeding or regular pillow for nursing, be aware that you might prop your baby up too high, preventing a good latch. Generally, your baby should be slightly lower than your breast.

Jocelyn Goodwin

However, a good breastfeeding pillow can be a great tool! You may want to use it:

- Behind your back for support
- To support your arms after your baby has latched
- To raise your arms if you have a longer torso, to prevent you from hunching over

If you choose to use a breastfeeding pillow, play around with different positions to find what's helpful and comfortable for you.

A Breastfeeding Bra

Breastfeeding bras are incredibly helpful when you're nursing your baby, but it's important to select the right kind of bra to prevent mastitis and blocked ducts.

- From 0-3 months: Choose a bra that's extremely stretchy and somewhat loose. It will be less supportive than a normal bra but necessary because your body is adapting to your milk levels and you don't want any constriction on your breasts that might cause your milk to coagulate.
- From 3-6 months: You can introduce a slightly more supportive bra that is still stretchy but can be worn when you want more support. Avoid underwire bras, push-up bras, sports bras, or any other compressive bras for the first 6 months.

Common Breastfeeding Ailments

Once you've established a successful breastfeeding relationship, feeding can be an incredible bonding experience, but many new moms, and even experienced moms, face a lot of challenges along the way.

DMER

Dysphoric Milk Ejection Reflex or DMER is an abrupt emotional swing that occurs in roughly 9% of breastfeeding moms just before milk is released. These negative emotions usually come out of nowhere right when your breast starts to tingle, and they can last from a few minutes to up to 10 minutes. Although these emotions can be intense, you will likely feel normal between milk letdowns.

The best way to cope with DMER is to acknowledge it and remind yourself that these emotions are only in your head. Blaming yourself and worrying about it can make things worse, so try to take a few deep breaths and wait for the feelings to pass.[6]

Pain

Most new moms are told that breastfeeding shouldn't hurt at all and that if there's any pain, they're doing it wrong. However, this isn't necessarily true. Even if you have a deep latch, it won't be painless all the time. Even moms who figure out breastfeeding very quickly will experience discomfort and nipple soreness for the first few days.

Initial Latch Pain

It's normal to experience intense pain for 30-40 seconds after the baby latches, but it should subside after that. If the pain doesn't subside, gently detach your baby from the breast and try again.

To break the latch, place 1 finger in the corner of your baby's mouth and gently push on your breast to break the suction. It is important to do this before pulling your baby off the breast to prevent your nipples from becoming sore, cracked, or bruised.

Don't try to ignore the pain and keep nursing with a poor latch. No matter how hungry or fussy your baby may be, just one nursing session with a bad latch can cause nipple trauma and make breastfeeding miserable for a week. Always break the latch and try again if you're in pain.

Nipple Trauma

Nipple trauma can be one of the most painful and challenging parts of breastfeeding. Unless you and your baby figure out breastfeeding right away, you will probably experience sore or cracked nipples. If this happens to you, remember that you're not failing – you're just learning.

A deep latch prevents sore nipples, so this ailment is a sign that something needs to be tweaked. The good news is that nipples heal pretty quickly, so even if you start off with a bad latch and experience sore or cracked nipples, if you can correct the latch, your nipples will soon heal.

Itchy nipples are another common ailment, and this is often due to the healing process. They are getting pulled, sucked, and wet many times a day, so even with a great latch, they can still become dry and irritated.

Moisturizing your nipples will provide relief and reduce further damage. There are plenty of nipple creams and butters out there that are breastfeeding-safe.

Vasospasms

If your baby pinches your nipple while feeding, this can cause the blood vessels that supply the nipple to spasm. Vasospasms can also occur if you have Raynaud's syndrome.

When you have vasospasms, you will often see your nipple change color due to blood restriction. It can be incredibly painful when your baby unlatches and the blood flows back into your nipple.[7]

Blocked Ducts & Mastitis

Too much milk or an imbalance of good and bad bacteria in your milk can cause pressure on the ducts or tubes that bring your milk to your nipple. This pressure causes the tubes to close, leading to blocked ducts. This typically happens in a portion of the breast, either at the nipple or further back in the duct system.

Since the milk isn't moving, pressure builds up behind the clogged duct and a portion of your breast will feel tender. You also might notice a triangle shape on your breast that is often hard and red. Initially, blocked ducts lead to engorgement, which can then lead to mastitis over time.

Mastitis typically starts with lumpy, sore, and swollen breasts. As the mammary glands become more inflamed, it can be very painful and may be accompanied by chills, a fever, and a racing heart. It essentially can feel like the flu without the congestion. You'll need to be treated with antibiotics if it gets to this point.[8]

You may also notice a small white spot called a white bleb on your nipple if a duct has been blocked at the end of the nipple. Some remedies are to roll your nipple, soak it in Epsom salt, and then gently rub it off. It might look like a white head on your nipple, but as tempting as it may be, don't try to pop it.

One of the best ways to prevent engorgement, blocked ducts, and mastitis is to frequently nurse. Going too long without removing milk from your breast can be a common cause of these ailments.

If a part of your breast feels full or lumpy, massage it while your baby is feeding. You can also hand express if your baby isn't due for a nursing session or you aren't with your baby.

Another tip for prevention is being aware of any seatbelt, bra, or over-body purse that may cut off the flow of milk.

Even with care and the best intentions, mastitis and blocked ducts are relatively common in the first 2-3 weeks after birth, but there are home remedies you can try. World-renowned lactation consultant Maya Bolman says that breast issues should be treated like swollen ankles. You want to focus on decreasing inflammation and swelling. Avoid using deep heat, as this makes your blood vessels dilate and swell. The same goes for deep massage.[9]

Instead, follow these steps to reduce inflammation:

1. Perform Maya Bolman's breast gymnastics. Very gently and slowly lift your breast with both hands, up and down, left and right. Next, make a circle, moving your breast clockwise a few times and then counter-clockwise a few times. Repeat the same with the other breast. Do this before each feeding as necessary.
2. Gently stroke from the breast toward the armpit to help lymphatic drainage. You can also apply some coconut or olive oil to the breast while doing this.
3. Breastfeed, pump, or hand express to release the extra milk.
4. Apply a cold compress after a feed.

Thrush

Thrush is a fungal infection often caught by breastfeeding mothers. It can be present on the mom or on the baby. If thrush is present in the baby's mouth, it often makes them fussy during feeding and you might notice white patches inside their mouth.

If thrush is on you, you will likely see itchy, flaky, or shiny skin on the nipple, areola, or breast. You might experience severe pain while breastfeeding, and it's sometimes hard to diagnose since the symptoms are often the same as a shallow latch. If you suspect you or your baby might have thrush, see a doctor for treatment options.[10]

Red Flags!

While there are many breastfeeding ailments that cause pain, there are some other red flags that indicate a breastfeeding issue. Here are some of the most common:

- Your baby sucks from 1 breast for a short period or only takes 2 or 3 sucks before falling asleep
- Your baby still seems hungry after feeding
- The fullness or hardness of your breasts doesn't decrease after feeding

These red flags could mean that your baby isn't getting a deep enough latch, so the sucking reflex isn't being triggered, and your baby is likely not getting enough milk. They could also be a sign that your baby doesn't have the strength and energy to feed well at the breast. Alternatively, they may be a sign of a tongue-tie, sucking issue, or another medical condition.

Tongue-Tie

A tongue-tie occurs when the baby's tongue can't move properly in the bottom of their mouth. Tongue-ties can impact breastfeeding, but they can be laser cut by an ear, nose, and throat doctor (ENT), which is a fairly simple procedure, and the baby can nurse right after. If you think this is an issue, it's important to get a tongue-tie assessment. Tongue-ties can also lead to other oral issues later if they aren't addressed.[11]

Low Supply

Since breastfeeding is all about supply and demand, the best way to increase your supply is to let your baby nurse frequently. Low supply is something many new moms worry about, but it's relatively uncommon for mothers to physically be unable to produce enough milk. If you think you may have a low supply, get help from your doctor, since this can be due to a number of medical conditions.

Three common causes of low supply are:

- Mom not drinking enough water
- A shallow latch cycle; if your baby has a shallow latch, your body will not increase your supply, leading to your baby not getting enough milk and not having enough energy to continue nursing. If this isn't addressed, the cycle will continue
- Skipping feedings or not putting your baby to the breast regularly

Assuming there's no underlying condition, there are ways to increase your milk supply, including:

- Keeping your diet high in protein, zinc, and calcium
- Drinking lots of water; keep a large water bottle with you while you're nursing to remind yourself to drink
- Focusing on achieving a deep latch and requesting help if necessary
- Incorporating breast compressions at the end of each feed on both breasts to help your baby get the fattiest milk
- Allowing your baby unrestricted access to your breasts. Don't try to schedule feedings, but let your baby nurse whenever they want
- Using a hospital-grade pump to pump after feeding (get guidance from a professional)[12]

Combination Feeding

If you're planning on breastfeeding, it's important not to offer a bottle too soon. Offering a bottle too soon can affect your milk production and your baby's willingness to feed from the breast.

It can be difficult being the only one capable of feeding your baby at first. When you're sleep-deprived and adjusting to life with a newborn, sometimes all you want is a break, but to establish a successful breastfeeding relationship, wait until at least 6 weeks postpartum to introduce a bottle. This gives you enough time to master the latch and establish the relationship, avoiding any confusion. In Chapter 5, we will discuss how to introduce the bottle without creating a nipple preference.

Pumping – Expressing Your Breast Milk

If you're expecting your little one very soon (or they've already arrived), you might be panicking if you don't have a pump yet. However, you'll notice that I didn't put it on the list of what you need before giving birth. There's certainly nothing wrong with getting a pump, especially if you are planning on going back to work, but a lot of women end up never using one. Before you buy a pump, figure out what you'll use it for and if it's really necessary. If you don't need it, it may be better to spend the money on a lactation consultant.

Here are some reasons why you may need to pump:

- Your baby has an issue with latching and you want to pump exclusively
- You are unwell or the baby is unwell. You can normally continue breastfeeding even if you or your baby are sick, but sometimes feeding may be too difficult
- You are returning to work at 8 weeks – in order to collect the maximum amount of milk, frequent pumping

sessions are better than long ones, and you should pump both breasts in the same session
- You're going away for a night or a day
- You're trying to build up your low milk supply under the guidance of a lactation specialist

If you determine that purchasing a breast pump is worth it, there are several kinds to choose from, including:

- Manual or hand pumps: these are for casual pumping, if you're pumping in between feeds occasionally. Manual or hand pumps aren't efficient for pumping consistently
- Electric and battery-operated pumps: most electric or battery-operated pumps automatically start with a massage mode and then switch to extraction after a few minutes. These are great for anyone who needs to pump on a regular basis. If you'll regularly need to pump somewhere without an outlet, be sure to invest in a battery-operated pump
- Hospital-grade pumps: these are normally used to build up a low milk supply and would be used to pump after a feeding

If you don't have a specific reason to pump, it's definitely not necessary. Any mom who has pumped knows that it involves a lot of work and hassle. Cleaning the pump and bottles alone takes up a lot of time.

Issues Related to Pumping

The more you empty your breasts, the more milk your breasts make, so if you are pumping, it's easy to get into a cycle of overproduction. Many moms end up throwing milk away, and overproduction can lead to engorgement, clogged ducts, or mastitis.

A high supply can often be harder and more painful to deal with than a low supply. It's discouraging to see your baby only drink a portion of what you are producing, and it can also make it difficult for your baby to nurse, because there is too much milk being let down at once. It's important not to cause your body to overproduce milk if you can avoid it.

Some moms choose to pump casually to build up a milk supply. If you need a supply for while you're at work, there may be times when you need to pump outside of typical feedings. However, casually pumping when you don't need to can lead to engorgement. If your body is used to you pumping once a day between feeds, you'll likely become engorged if you go a day without doing so.

Other moms choose to pump to avoid nighttime feedings. Perhaps you have decided to build up a supply so your partner can give your baby a bottle at night, allowing you to get some much-needed rest. Unfortunately, while this might sound attractive, it can cause problems.

Not feeding at night will likely lower your milk supply. The milk-making hormone, prolactin, is higher at night. If your breasts are not stimulated or emptied overnight, your prolactin will not spike, leading to a lower supply the next day. This is important to consider.

Another issue with pumping relates to suction pumps. Suction pumps are an option that some moms use when they want to collect milk during a feed. The idea is that you attach the pump to 1 breast while your baby is feeding on the other, and the pump collects milk that would otherwise be wasted in a breast pad.

The problem with this method is that the only milk collected is foremilk – the thinner milk that sits at the front of the ducts. This is rich in lactose, which is harder for your little one to digest, and it might lead to a gassy baby with green and frothy poops.

However, a suction pump can be helpful for moms with an oversupply or forceful letdown. You can use the suction pump to empty the breast a little bit, making it easier for your baby to latch and swallow the milk.

Pumping is Hard Work!

If it's necessary for you to pump due to going back to work or latch issues, it's great to have the option, but if it's not necessary, think about how much work is involved before you purchase a pump. Yes, it's challenging to never have a break from feeding your baby, but breastfeeding, pumping, and bottle-feeding (also known as triple feeding) can be even more work. I applaud moms who do this.

However, before you decide to pump, think about why you're doing it and proceed with caution until your supply is regulated, at around 8-12 weeks.

When All Else Fails

There's no way around it: breastfeeding is a tough job! It may be natural, but it doesn't come easily to everyone. If you struggle, remember that it doesn't mean you're failing or that there's something wrong with you. Any breastfeeding mom will tell you just how challenging it is, especially in the beginning.

Everyone's anatomy is different, and not everything you see in videos or textbooks will work for you. There are many factors that contribute to success. It takes most women 6-8 weeks to fully establish breastfeeding, so be determined and remember to ask for help from a specialist if you need to. There is a great deal of value in having a professional or experienced person watch you breastfeed to help you correct any issues. In many cases, it's an easy fix. The most important thing is to get help when necessary and not give up.

5

No Nonsense Bottle-feeding

To successfully bottle feed, all you need is formula or milk and a bottle, right? Well, not exactly. If you want a successful bottle-feeding experience, know that there's more to it than just filling a bottle with milk and feeding your baby.

Many new moms cannot breastfeed or choose not to for various reasons, and whether you're supplementing with formula, giving bottles of stored breast milk, or full-on formula feeding, most babies will feed from a bottle at some point.

According to the CDC, 42.6% of breastfed 6-month-olds are supplemented with formula at least some of the time.[1] Babies are unable to digest cow's milk until they're a year old, so even if you start by breastfeeding, your infant will need either breast milk or formula until their first birthday.

Like breastfeeding, getting into a routine with bottle-feeding can seem overwhelming. It can make keeping your baby nourished a lot more work. However, once you find a formula your baby likes, you'll soon settle into a good feeding routine. You might be surprised by how quickly making formula bottles becomes second nature, and you'll even be able to do it in the middle of the night.

Although there may be fewer challenges to bottle-feeding, it isn't always easy. Unfortunately, the media has skewed our view of what bottle-feeding should look like. When we picture a baby bottle-feeding, we typically imagine a baby lying flat with the bottle upright. This is called gravity-led bottle-feeding. This means the bottle releases milk whether the baby wants it to or not, and they have to keep swallowing in order to breathe, leading to them guzzling the milk down.

In an ideal world, we want bottle-feeding to mimic the pace and patterns of breastfeeding as much as possible.

Basics of Bottle-feeding

When it comes to newborn bottle-feeding, what you need depends on how often your baby will drink from a bottle. If you are exclusively bottle-feeding, I recommend you have around 8-12 bottles to rotate through. This will make feeding simpler since newborns eat every 2-3 hours. If you are supplementing some of the time, 3-4 bottles will suffice.

One of the most overwhelming parts of establishing your bottle-feeding routine is finding the right bottles. You might have a specific one that you have researched and added to your registry, but there are many different brands, and all of them make different claims about preventing gas or colic, or about looking and smelling like a breast. You might start to wonder if your baby will even take a bottle if you choose the wrong one.

The best answer is to try a variety of bottles and nipples. No matter what each manufacturer claims, many babies have a preference, so what works for one baby might not work for another.

In the beginning, avoid buying bottles or nipples in bulk. Try lots of different bottles and brands until you find the one that works best for your baby and you. Every baby is different, so it will likely take some trial and error to find the right nipple shape and length. Regardless of what anyone tells you, the best bottle is the one your baby will drink from.

When selecting bottles, keep in mind that it is important that the bottle is comfortable for you to hold, and newborns should always start using a slow flow nipple, often called a level or stage 1 nipple, or a newborn nipple.

There are several different types of formula options, so choose what works best for you and your lifestyle. When looking into types of formulas, you'll find:

- Powdered formula: you add water to the powder. This is typically the most affordable option
- Concentrated, liquid formula: you add water here as well
- Premixed, ready-to-use formula: this type is ready to go once you open it. There's no need to add water, but it is the most expensive option. However, it's great on the go, and is typically recommended for babies with impaired immune systems or preemies, because it is sterilized

All types of formulas sold have to abide by the USDA Nutrition Standards, so try not to get bogged down by the brand.[2] Use what works best for your baby. You also don't need to stress if you end up switching brands. Breast milk changes daily based on a mother's diet, so changes in formula are okay too. Talk to your healthcare provider about which formula might be best for you and your baby, especially if you have any concerns.

Amount & Time

When it comes to breastfeeding, you don't have to think as much about how many ounces your baby is drinking, but when you're bottle-feeding, you want to ensure you're offering your baby enough.

Here are some general guidelines for how much your baby will eat from birth to 6 months:

- First 7 days after birth: 1-2 ounces per feed. You can offer a bottle every 2-4 hours. Keep track of the number of wet diapers to ensure they eat enough.
- First 30 days: the amount of formula gradually increases until they take around 3-4 ounces per feed. Continue to offer a bottle every 2-4 hours.
- 2 months to 6 months: The amount they consume should level out around 4-6 ounces per feed and they will likely go 4-5 hours between bottles.[3]

The AAP recommends roughly 2.5 ounces (or 75ml) a day per pound of body weight for babies from 5 days to 6 months.[4] Your baby will regulate from day to day to meet their specific needs. Remember, these are guidelines to follow, but no book or website can tell you exactly how much you should feed your baby and how often. In fact, the amount of formula recommended varies from country to country. These numbers should be a ballpark for you, not a guarantee.

Each feed should take around 15-30 minutes. If your baby finishes in 5-10 minutes, you'll need to slow down their feedings.

Now that you know what to expect, let's discuss what you need to know if you'll be formula feeding from day 1.

Formula Feeding From the Start

No matter what your reason is, feeding your baby formula doesn't make you a bad mom, but there are some things you need to know if this is the path you're taking from your baby's birth.

First off, let's explore what you can expect at the hospital. They will likely supply formula in ready-to-go bottles during your hospital stay. You are welcome to switch formula brands when you get home and it's typical for many moms to do so. Don't feel pressured to stick with the formula they gave your baby at the hospital. During the newborn phase, you can change the formula immediately, rather than transitioning gradually.

It's best practice to bring the hospital bottles home with you. The bottles they provide are the perfect size for your baby during the first few weeks.

Preparation

Once you're home, the feeding process can seem overwhelming at times. You will quickly learn that when it comes to stress-free bottle-feeding, preparation is everything. It can also be helpful to decide how you are going to clean the bottles and which water you want to use ahead of time.

Sterilization is a widely debated topic, and the idea that you need to frequently sterilize bottles comes from the times when water supplies weren't reliably clean. In today's world, assuming your water supply isn't harboring dangerous bacteria, it's unnecessary.[5]

Additionally, once the bottle or nipple is exposed to air, it's going to pick up germs from the environment, so in most cases, it's not going to be completely sterile anyway. It is also important to note that all formula contains a warning that it is not sterile and that once it is opened, it may be contaminated in your kitchen. No matter how much you clean, our environments are full of germs, so don't stress too much about sterilization. Use hot, soapy water to clean bottles, nipples, pacifiers, and other feeding supplies; this should be all you need to do.

What water to use is another widely debated topic. Purified bottled water is often the easiest option since you don't have to boil it. It is important to choose bottled water that's low in sodium (less than 200 mg per liter) and sulfate (less than 250 mg per liter).[6]

If you do use tap water, since it's convenient and free, let the water run for around 2 minutes before filling up your pot. Once the water is boiling, let it boil for at least 1 minute, and then cool it to room temperature. Once your water has cooled, use it straight away. Avoid leaving water sitting out for over 30 minutes and then using it for a bottle.[7]

Whether you use bottled or tap water, save yourself some time by introducing room temperature milk or formula to your baby from the beginning. There's no health reason to use warm formula, and if your baby is used to drinking it at room temperature, they won't demand it any other way. If you do prefer to warm it, always test the temperature of the formula by putting a few drops on the inside of your wrist.

Before making a bottle, always check the integrity and expiration date of the formula. Formula can lose nutritional value quickly if the seal is broken or it's past the expiration date.

For the safety of your little one, it's important to closely follow the instructions on the formula packaging. It's true that formula can be expensive, and with the other costs of being a new mom, it can be tempting to water down the formula. Equally, if you feel your baby isn't gaining enough weight, it can be tempting to add more than the correct measurement to increase calories. Both scenarios are dangerous. Though your intentions may be good, improper formula concentration can irritate your baby's delicate digestive system.

Once you've checked the integrity of the formula and gotten your measurements, it's time to prepare your bottle:

1. Add the desired amount of water and then add the corresponding amount of formula powder or concentrated liquid
2. Place the nipple and lid on the bottle and give it a good shake (rather than stirring it) to evenly distribute powder or concentrate
3. Offer the prepared formula at room temperature within 2 hours of mixing it. If you're not planning on using the bottle right away, store the prepared formula in the fridge ASAP and serve within 24 hours to prevent contamination

If you want to skip these steps, you can buy a formula mixer. It's sort of like a Keurig but for formula! If you plan on exclusively formula feeding, it may save you a lot of time in the long run.

Getting Started!

Now it's time to get started. Parents often think their babies are too young to understand their needs and wants. However, they fail to realize that babies are never too young to know exactly what they need to eat, how much to eat, or when to eat. Babies can recognize whether they are hungry or full. This will make your life easier, so trust it.

As a parent, it's easy to look at charts and count ounces, and I understand that relying on your baby's cues may be hard, particularly when you have a newborn and you are worried that they aren't getting enough calories. However, if your baby is showing signs of not wanting to eat, rest assured that it's okay for you to skip a few feeds until they get hungry and want to eat again.

Unless your baby is preterm or has a physical condition that is interfering with their ability to feed, you need to trust that they are capable of self-regulating their intake. Almost all babies will be able to meet their nutritional requirements, growth, and energy needs if you allow them to control their intake.

If you're unsure, consider breastfed babies. How much they consume is entirely directed by the baby. There's no way for the parents to have any control over how much their baby eats, and in most cases, they're not even sure how many ounces the baby is eating. This means the baby relies on instinct to determine how much to eat and, most importantly, when to stop eating. This is why the internal hunger cues for breastfed babies tend to be well-developed.[8]

However, bottle-fed babies don't normally have the chance to direct their feeding, and instead, parents tend to follow guidelines that lead to overfeeding. For example, if their babies don't finish the bottle, the parents usually force or encourage them to finish. This can present many problems in the future, including an aversion to the bottle. This is why it's so important to know and understand your baby's feeding cues.

As the parent, your only responsibility is to offer food and a relaxed environment. It's up to your baby to decide:

- When to feed
- How much to feed
- When to stop feeding
- Whether to feed at all[9]

Paced Bottle-Feeding or Baby-Led Feeding

There are several different ways to feed a baby a bottle. Paced bottle-feeding or baby-led feeding is a technique used to slow down the flow of milk during a bottle-feeding session.

This technique is designed to mimic breastfeeding and has many benefits, including:

- The baby is in control of how much formula they're consuming
- The baby can develop the cues of hunger and satiety, which are crucial to healthy eating later in life
- The baby won't eat too quickly, reducing the risk of gas
- The baby will develop all their oral facial muscles
- The baby is at less risk of choking and coughing
- The baby is at less risk of ear infections

This feeding method is recommended for any baby that receives bottles, whether fully bottle-fed or fed from the breast and a bottle. To successfully pace feed your baby, you will need to pay attention to your baby's position, how you offer the bottle, and how you conduct the feeding session. So, let's get started!

When getting your baby into a position to bottle feed, avoid "crook of the arm" positioning because the bottle nipple will be angled down and gravity will be doing all the work. The positions that allow the baby to control the flow of milk are:

Upright position- baby is sitting on your lap facing outwards toward the room or facing sideways

Side-lying position- You're sitting with your knees bent and feet propped up, or your legs crossed. Baby is lying on their side with their head closest to your knees. Their head should be higher than their feet.

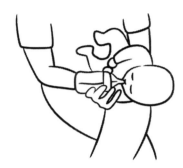

Note: Swaddling or any other restrictive positions should be avoided during feeding time. You want to ensure your baby's hands are free. Your baby's hands will give you various cues, including signs of distress or discomfort. It's important for you to gauge their movements and reactions so you can respond properly.

Both you and your baby should be comfortable during each feeding session. It's okay and encouraged to snuggle up with your baby while feeding. You want your baby to feel supported, so have them in a secure position so there's no risk of falling, and always support their back and neck. Position yourself with pillows under your arms, back, or anywhere else you may need them.

Once your baby is in the proper position, you can offer the bottle. Start by asking your baby's permission. You can do this by tickling their nose or top and bottom lip with the nipple, then waiting for their mouth to open. This motivates your baby to take the lead in latching onto the nipple.

Aim the bottle nipple up when it goes into their mouth to trigger the sucking reflex. You want the whole nipple to be in their mouth so all the muscles are being used, not just their lips. Their lips should look flared like a fish around the widest part of the nipple base.

Keep the bottle horizontal so your baby has to actively suck to draw out the milk. The nipple should only be partially full of milk and you want to see milk at the end of the nipple, with an air bubble toward the back.

As the baby sucks, don't push the bottle into their mouth. Instead, keep it neutral or tension it away from the baby's mouth, as if you are gently playing tug of war to trigger the baby to pull the nipple deep into their mouth.

Take a break when you see any of the following:

- The baby is swallowing without taking breaths – look for a breath every 3-5 sucks
- Milk is spilling out of their mouth
- Their nostrils are flaring
- Their eyes are wide
- Their arms/legs are stiff
- Their toes and fingers are splayed
- Their lips are turning blue
- They're fussy[10]

In these moments, you can take a break for a few seconds by dropping the bottle slightly with the nipple still in their mouth. This allows them to keep sucking but gives them a break from the milk. You can also break the suction and remove the nipple if they're fussy and need a burp.

If you haven't taken a break by a quarter of the way through a feed because they haven't signaled for one, take one anyway and offer a burp.

Halfway through the feed, alternate sides so you're feeding in both arms. This prevents your baby from preferring a single feeding side and helps stimulate both sides of the baby's body and eyes.

Even if it seems easier, never prop up a bottle and always watch your baby so you can respond to their cues. Propping up a bottle increases the incidences of ear infections.[11]

Take your time and continue to take pauses when your baby signals. It's important for you to be an active part of the feeding process. It takes time for your baby to feel full, so if you rush through the feeding, there's a higher chance of overfeeding and having a fussy baby later on.

Ending a Feed

It is best to end a feed when your baby is full and this should never be based on if they have finished the bottle or not. If your baby is full, they may be:

- Turning their head away
- Pressing their lips together
- Letting go of the nipple
- No longer sucking
- Thrusting the tongue out of the mouth
- Falling asleep

Recognizing their cues and ending the feeding when they're full helps to establish healthy eating habits.

Always offer a burp when your baby has finished. It's not always easy to find the best position for burping your baby, but be patient and remember that most bottle-fed babies will need 2-3 burps per feeding. Burping techniques are discussed more in Chapter 7.

Some moms choose not to do paced feeding because the baby typically swallows more air than during traditional feeding, but remember any air in the stomach that causes discomfort can come up as a burp. Trapped wind or farts are caused by digestion, not air ingested while feeding.

After a Feed

When you've ended the feeding session, babies who excessively spit up will benefit from upright movement for 30 minutes. This movement could be gentle rocking or bouncing to help them digest their food.[12]

It may be helpful to give the bottle a quick rinse with warm water to get rid of the leftover residue. Later, come back and thoroughly wash the full day's worth of bottles. This will save you from having to wash bottles repeatedly throughout the day.

You can purchase a special dishwasher basket for all the bottle pieces if you choose, so you can keep nipples, collars, valves, etc., in one place and not all over the dishwasher. It's also useful to have a bottle brush and drying rack specifically for the bottles.

If there's any formula left at the end of a feed, it's safest to throw it out since the combination of baby saliva and formula can prompt bacteria to grow in the bottle.[13] Saving a little bit of money isn't worth the risk of your baby getting sick.

Common Pitfalls with Newborns

Even though bottle-feeding can seem straightforward, there are some pitfalls, especially with newborns. Babies are born with an automatic sucking reflex that is functional for the first 6-8 weeks of their lives, making it extremely easy for parents to overfeed and the baby to end up with an upset stomach. When the roof of the baby's mouth is touched, the baby will start to suck whether they are hungry or not.[14]

Once they are 2-3 months old, their sucking reflex starts to fade, which means they can turn down a feeding session if they want. Parents sometimes become alarmed when their baby suddenly refuses the bottle, and they might go into panic mode.

This can lead to parents using tactics to trick the baby into eating more than the baby wants, such as:

- Making repeated offers for them to eat
- Restraining the baby's head and arms during a feeding session
- Following their baby's head around with the bottle
- Jiggling the bottle around
- Touching their face
- Squeezing the milk into the baby's mouth
- Introducing distractions like toys

Most parents don't realize they're forcing their baby to eat. They might be concerned that their child isn't getting enough nutrition or gaining enough weight. However, the truth is, every baby will eat different amounts and these amounts change over time. One baby might have multiple small feeds spread throughout the day, and another might enjoy only a few feeding sessions where they drink the entire bottle. Both ways can provide all the required nutrition.

Force-feeding is a serious problem that many parents who bottle-feed from day 1 face and it can easily turn into bottle-feeding aversion.

There are other issues that might also affect your bottle-feeding, such as:

Bottle Ring

If the bottle you're using has a bottle ring, it's important not to screw it on too tight. The bottle ring balances the pressure in a non-vented bottle, which is important for optimizing the flow rate. If insufficient air can enter the bottle during the feeding, it becomes very difficult for your baby to get any milk out of the bottle. The tightness of the bottle ring can be the difference between a successful or unsuccessful feed, so it's crucial that you see a steady flow of bubbles into the bottle as your baby eats.

Mold

It's easy for mold to grow on moist objects, making bottles a target for this fungus. This is especially common if the bottles you're using have valves. Due to this risk, it's important to do routine cleaning and inspect your bottles to ensure they dry thoroughly before storing them.

The bottles and bottle parts should be taken apart and cleaned thoroughly after each feed, and you should throw away any old bottles or nipples that are cloudy, cracked, scratched, or sticky.

Mold will affect the taste of the formula. If it becomes a constant issue, consider purchasing single-use disposable nipples and disposable liner bottles.

Faulty Equipment

Regular wear and tear can make bottles and nipples malfunction over time. A good rule of thumb is to replace the nipples every 2 months. However, you should check the bottle and nipple before each use regardless of how long you've been using them.

You can check for faulty equipment by testing the nipple drip rate. To do this test, hold the bottle upside down. Ideally, the milk from the bottle should drip at the rate of 1 drop per second.[15] If the drip rate is off, that's an indication that something is wrong with your feeding equipment.

Taste & Consistency of the Milk

It's possible that your baby might not like the taste of the formula. You can try switching to a different brand and see if that does the trick, although it's recommended that you try a new formula for 2 weeks before giving up on it.

If your baby is taking any kind of medication, it can leave a nasty aftertaste in their mouth. It is best not to give your baby any medication directly before a feed.

It is also common for parents to fail to mix the formula thoroughly. If the formula has an uneven consistency, the baby might slowly become averse to the bottle.

Allergies

The most common allergy seen in bottle-fed babies is a cow's milk protein allergy, where the baby's immune system reacts unusually to the protein found in cow's milk. It's estimated that this type of allergy affects 0.5% of breastfed babies and 2-7.5% of formula fed.[16] Babies with cow's milk protein allergy can present symptoms such as:

- Reflux
- Vomiting
- Nausea
- Constipation
- Trapped gas
- Excessive farting

If your baby is suffering from CMPA or intolerance to milk, you'll likely see signs of the allergy during the first 4 weeks of life. Always talk with your doctor before switching to a hypoallergenic formula without cow's milk protein. These typically don't taste as good as normal formulas, so it won't incentivize your baby to drink more milk, and should only be given if they are actually allergic to cow's milk.[17]

Baby Is Gagging

Some babies might have a hyper-sensitive gag reflex. If you do notice your baby gagging often, the shaft of the nipple might be too long for them.

Baby Is Chewing on the Nipple

This mostly happens as babies get older. They often do this when they're not hungry, and they see it as a game. If you notice your baby chewing on the nipple, end the feeding session and play with them instead of trying to feed them.

Same Caregiver Doing Every Feed

One of the biggest benefits of bottle-feeding is that the mom isn't the only one who can feed the baby. Take advantage of this by encouraging other family members to get involved. When parents, grandparents, and other loved ones take turns with the bottle, your baby will adapt to new positions and feeding will become part of their positive social environment.

Bottle-Feeding Over the Next Few Months

As your baby gets bigger, their feeding preferences will change and you might have to transition to a nipple with a faster flow rate.

Here are some signs that the flow rate of the bottle is too slow:

- The baby is taking an unusually long time to finish drinking (between 30-45 minutes)
- The baby is falling asleep in the middle of drinking

- The baby is becoming frustrated or aggravated while drinking. They may be squirming, kicking, or pushing the bottle away
- The baby is sucking hard
- The baby is flattening the nipple[18]

If you're currently using a Level 1 nipple and your baby is showing any or all of these signs, go to a Level 2 nipple and look for the signs again. Your baby will likely not need a Level 3 nipple until 6 months or older.

Here are some signs that the flow rate of the bottle is too fast:

- The baby's eyebrows go up during a feeding in a startled way
- The baby has clenched fists or brings their fists up to their face
- The baby is frowning or looks worried
- The baby is pulling back from the bottle
- The baby is coughing, spluttering, or choking
- The baby is having difficulty swallowing
- The baby is gulping
- There's milk dripping from baby's mouth while feeding
- The baby is refusing the bottle altogether[19]

It can also be helpful to get bigger bottles as your baby's formula consumption increases with age. Most newborn bottles are 4 ounces. Larger bottles, typically around 8-9 ounces, can be helpful when your baby is around 4 months old, or you may use one sooner if your baby is drinking more than 4 ounces per feed.

Transitioning From Breast to Bottle: Full or Partial Weaning

There are many reasons why you may need to transition your baby to a bottle, and sometimes, you may need to transition them quickly. It's natural for your baby to resist this transition at first, so understand that this is a common part of the process.

After all, babies who breastfeed feel warm and comforted at their mother's breast, and it allows them to stay close to you. From the baby's perspective, the bottle is a foreign object that they're confused about.

Let's go over everything you need to keep in mind to give your baby a smooth and enjoyable transition from the breast to the bottle. These solutions are based on the assumption that your baby already has healthy breastfeeding habits and no other feeding issues.

Breast vs. Bottle

Breastfeeding and bottle-feeding call for completely different mechanisms, patterns, and tongue movements, which is why babies sometimes struggle to transition from one to the other.

Breastfeeding works by nipple stimulation- when the baby releases oxytocin, your milk is let down. If the baby wants more, they'll do it again. It generally takes longer to breastfeed because breast milk is let down in cycles that start and stop. It's not a continuous flow. Bottle-feeding is a lot easier for babies, but it does take time to get used to if the baby wasn't bottle-fed from birth.

Nipple Confusion or Nipple Preference

One of the main concerns moms have about using a bottle too soon or having to use a bottle temporarily is nipple confusion, also known as nipple preference. Your baby uses a different technique to remove milk from the breast than when they drink from a bottle and your baby will have established a suck-swallow-breathe pattern unique to the flow of milk from the breast if that's what they're used to.

The bottle and nipple that you use can make a difference, but it may take some trial and error to find the one that works for your baby. Regardless of how old your breastfed baby is, the slow-flow nipple, or newborn nipple, is going to best mimic the manner in which milk flows from the breast. You might have to try a few brands before finding the best fit for your baby.

It can be tempting to only purchase ones that claim to look and feel like a breast, but focus instead on ones that have a long, straight nipple at the end, with a gentle slope to the wider base. These are good for a deep latch. Anything that's working for you and your baby and allowing them to get a deep latch is great, even if it isn't marketed toward breastfed babies.

Some babies have difficulty alternating between a bottle and the breast, while others can go back and forth easily. If you decide to introduce a bottle, it's possible for your baby to develop a preference for the bottle over the breast during the transition phase. This is typically because the milk is a lot easier to get out of the bottle, and in this situation, your baby might end up rejecting the breast altogether.

If it's important to you that your baby continues to breastfeed, this isn't an ideal situation, so let's talk about a method that will help your baby switch back and forth.

Steps for Transitioning Your Baby to a Bottle

1. Wait for at least 6 weeks or until you have mastered your latch before introducing a bottle. If you wait till 8-9 months, skip the bottle entirely and go straight to a cup.

2. Plan ahead: it's important not to make this transition suddenly. You need to ease your baby into the process of bottle-feeding. Of course, life happens and sometimes it's not by choice that you need to transition your baby, but if you're anticipating separation from your baby in the near future, you might want to start offering the bottle at least 2 weeks in advance. This provides enough time for your baby to adjust to the bottle-feeding process and allows you time to deal with any feeding issues that might come up.

3. Let them explore the nipple on their own terms. Place the nipple with their toys or give it to them to play with. If they're old enough, they might even bring it to their mouth and suck on it like a pacifier. It can be scary for them if you place a strange thing in their mouth without warning. The goal is to make it safe, familiar, and non-threatening.

4. Start with a happy baby: the best way to start a bottle-feeding session is with a baby who is not too tired or hungry.

5. Prepare the milk: put breast milk or formula in a bottle with a slow-flow nipple. Keep in mind that breast milk tastes very different from formula. Pumping your own breast milk might make this transition easier than offering formula right away.

- With breast milk that has been frozen, thaw and properly warm the milk. Remember never to microwave breast milk! Frozen breast milk can be thawed in the refrigerator for over 12 hours or by holding the frozen bottle or bag under warm running water. It is also advised to use breastmilk from the same time of day since breastmilk in the evening has more melatonin.
- If you're using formula, it can be helpful to rub some of your breast milk on the outside of the nipple to entice the baby to drink.

6. Think about position: for previously breastfed babies, it can be best to hold them facing outwards toward the room. Use gentle movements when holding the baby in this position. You can also try:

- Rocking, bouncing, swaying, or walking around the room to stimulate your baby to take the bottle.
- Placing your baby in a bouncy seat, swing, or car seat to provide extra stimulation might also help.

Remember, you're not trying to trick your baby into taking the bottle, but instead, you're providing positive reinforcement to motivate them to drink from it.

7. Follow the paced feeding technique that was covered previously, and ensure your baby has a deep latch. You don't want your baby to suck from the bottle with a shallow latch and get the milk with little effort, or it will be harder to get them to take the breast again. Whether they're sucking on the end of the nipple or have a deep latch, they'll get the same amount of milk, but having a shallow latch doesn't use as many muscles. This is the most important step for helping your baby easily switch between the breast and the bottle.

If the baby accepts the bottle and you want to partially wean them, do the next 2-3 feedings from your breast before introducing the bottle again. If you want to switch to formula completely, keep offering formula for the next feeding.

If the baby rejects the bottle, remember that this is okay and pretty common. It can be difficult and frustrating when this happens, but keep offering the bottle in a gentle, non-pressuring way. This will help you get results much faster than forcing them to take the bottle, leading to them refusing it in the future.

Try offering the bottle up to a maximum of 3 times during any given feeding time. If your baby continues to refuse the bottle again and again, it's crucial that you don't offer the breast immediately after they refuse the bottle. This can lead to them thinking they're being rewarded for refusing the bottle.

If you're still struggling to transition your baby, here are some other things you can try:

- Play around with the milk's temperature: some breastfed babies prefer warm formula, while others prefer it cold. Try both and see which temperature your little one prefers.
- Heat the nipple up before offering it to your baby. This often makes your baby more receptive to the nipple, since it will mimic the warmth and comfort your baby receives at the breast.
- Rooting reflex: if you find your baby is struggling to take the bottle in their mouth, try triggering their rooting reflex by gently stroking their cheek or the corner of their mouth with the nipple of the bottle. This will trigger the baby to turn their head and open their mouth to follow the direction of the stroking.
- Have someone else offer the bottle: one of the benefits of transitioning to a bottle is that it allows the rest of the family to interact and bond with the baby. Your baby can smell the milk inside you, which may confuse them, since they don't understand why you aren't breastfeeding them. You can solve this issue by leaving the house while another familiar person takes over the feeding session. You can even wrap the bottle with a piece of your clothing so that your baby can smell a familiar scent. This may help your baby to remain calm and peaceful instead of being agitated over your absence.
- Timing: your baby might not be receptive to the bottle all times of the day. Usually, the best time to offer the bottle for the first few days is after your baby has completed

their normal feeding in the evening. However, you can try offering the bottle at different times and see how your baby responds. If they don't take the bottle during the day when they're alert, it's okay to initially offer the bottle when your baby is sleepy or tired as long as they have healthy breastfeeding habits during the day.

- Use hunger: it's okay to use hunger as a motivator by lessening the calories your baby receives from the breast. Reducing the calories obtained from your breast will increase your baby's willingness to take the bottle to satisfy their hunger. Don't wait until your baby is starving, but let them be hungry enough to accept the bottle.
- Place the bottle under your armpit: if having your baby facing outwards isn't working for you, try placing the bottle as close to the breast as possible, since this is where the baby is used to being fed. This is especially helpful for babies who really like to cuddle.

No matter what your current feeding situation is, transitioning from breast to bottle is going to be a slow, gradual process. Remember to allow your baby to take their time with the bottle. There should never be any pressure to feed from the bottle, just gentle and positive encouragement.

Continue to comfort your baby throughout the process, and try to enjoy the transition! If you're stressed during the feeding, your baby will pick up on that. It's okay to have fun with it. Try to find a way to make it an enjoyable time for you and your baby.

6

The A, B, Zzzz of Sleep

Newborn sleep is one of the most controversial topics you'll come across as a new mom. Everyone seems to have an opinion, and they're often pretty strong opinions. It's important to know what normal sleep looks like for a newborn, how to help them sleep safely, how to soothe a crying baby, and how to survive the night. It's also important to remember that every baby is different and what you think will work might go out the window once your baby arrives. You can know what to expect and what's normal, but be flexible too.

So let's talk about newborn sleep!

Is Sleeping Through the Night a Myth?

In those early days of being a new mom, you can pretty much guarantee you're going to run into another mom who will boast about their baby sleeping through the night, typically at a very young age. Go ahead and cue the eye roll. Comments like this often lead new moms to ask two questions. 1) Am I doing something wrong? 2) Are these newborn babies really sleeping 8-12 hours straight?

The short answer is, most likely not. For most babies from birth to 3 months, it's normal and healthy for them to wake up through the night. Generally, babies are not capable of sleeping for 6-8 hour stretches at night until they're at least 4-6 months old. At this stage, if your baby sleeps 4-5 hours straight, consider that a win.

The truth is, no matter how much or how little their baby sleeps, every new parent is tired. Feeding your baby around the clock and dealing with nighttime wakeups equals exhausted parents. The bad news is that newborn sleep is complex and varies from baby to baby, so there's no single trick that will get every baby to sleep. Any parents of twins or multiple children will tell you that. Babies who start off sleeping through the night often have trouble sleeping later on, and vice versa. Just when you think you've got it figured out, their sleep patterns tend to change.

No matter how challenging it is at first, they will eventually sleep for longer stretches, so hang on during those early days. Here's a typical range for how much you can expect your baby to sleep, depending on their age:

- Newborn: 16-18 hours per day
- 2 weeks-2 months: 15-17 hours per day
- 3 months-6 months: Around 15 hours per day

Remember that this will be broken sleep, not completed in one stretch.

Safe Sleep

Of course, one of the most important things to know before bringing your baby home is sleep safety. First, choose where your baby will sleep. Here are some of the most common guidelines for safe sleep:

- Have your baby sleep in a crib, bassinet, or pack 'n play
- Be aware that sidecar cribs attached to the bed or co-sleeper bassinets with a drop-down side have a higher risk of infant entrapment and bedding suffocation
- Find a mattress that is firm, flat, and the right size for your baby's crib. There shouldn't be room for more than the width of 2 adult fingers between your baby's mattress and the frame
- Use a waterproof mattress protector to make cleanups easier
- For the bedding, use a fitted sheet. Remove all blankets, pillows, bumper pads, soft toys, etc., from the baby's bed
- Babies should be placed to sleep on their back on a firm, flat sleeping surface. Using an incline, swing, rocker, or prop comes with an increased risk of SIDS and is not recommended by the AAP
- Keep your baby warm with a swaddle, wearable blanket, and/or one-piece sleeper[1]

Safe Co-sleeping/Bed Sharing

Co-sleeping is one of those things that brings in the unwanted cavalry. If you're considering co-sleeping, prepare for hundreds of doctors and other parents to quickly shame you and tell you how unsafe it is. However, it's estimated that 61% of babies bedshare at least some of the time.[2] So, is it really as unsafe as some people claim?

Most new mothers today don't plan to bedshare, especially with the strict safe sleep guidelines provided by numerous organizations. However, whether they plan to or not, a large

Jocelyn Goodwin

majority of moms will bedshare at some point, so it's important to discuss how to safely co-sleep.

Remember that co-sleeping isn't all bad. It's natural to want to keep your baby close to you at night. During our evolution, there would have been no such thing as a crib, and your baby would have been held or next to you at all times to protect them from threats. The data shows that co-sleeping positively influences your baby's heart rate, brain waves, sleep states, oxygen levels, temperature, and breathing.[3]

If someone brings up the dangers of co-sleeping, keep in mind that bed-sharing casualties are almost always associated with:

- Parents who have been smoking, drinking alcohol, or taking drugs (including over-the-counter medication)
- Babies who were placed on their stomachs
- Babies who were placed on a pillow
- Other children or pets being in the bed with the baby
- Sleeping on a sofa or armchair[4]

Safe Co-sleeping Tips

If you decide to co-sleep at some point in your parenting journey, both partners need to be on board and aware that the baby is sleeping in the bed. Additionally:

- You should only co-sleep in a firm bed, never on a sofa, recliner, or upholstered chair
- Your baby should not sleep in between partners, but instead on one side of the bed. If possible, have only one partner sleep with the baby
- Sleep on your side with your knees bent so you cannot roll over onto your baby. Imagine you are making a C position with your body around the baby

104

- You should only co-sleep if you're completely sober. Don't smoke, drink, or do drugs before co-sleeping, even if they're over-the-counter drugs that make you drowsy
- Tie up long hair if necessary
- Remove all blankets, pillows, and sheets that are near the baby and cover up any cracks in the bed
- Make sure the baby is lying on their back[5]

How to Put a Baby to Sleep

Babies can quickly become impossible to manage when they are not getting enough sleep. On top of that, you will spend most of your time as a new mom settling your baby to sleep, so it is essential to master this in order to maintain some sanity.

Recognize Sleep Cues

Newborns get tired very quickly. It's important to look for cues that it is time to start settling them down. Look out for the following signs:

- Zoning out and startling back to attention

- Yawning
- Wide-eyed stare
- Arms and legs jerking around wildly
- Rubbing their eyes
- Pulling their ears
- Distraught cries
- Sighing or grunting
- Turning their head from side to side
- White-knuckled grip with fists
- Disengaged with no eye contact[6]

Recreate the Womb

Recreating the womb is a great way to soothe a crying newborn back to sleep. Harvey Karp, author of *The Happiest Baby on the Block,* found that "the !Kung San of the Kalahari Desert mothers usually calm their fussy babies in under a minute! Their secret? The !Kung mothers hold their infants almost 24 hours a day, constantly feeding, rocking, and jiggling them. In essence, they mimic the womb experience for months."[7]

With that in mind, Dr. Karp put together the 5 S's: Swaddle, Side, Shhh, Suck, and Swing. These 5 things keep the baby relaxed because it's the rhythm they experienced in the womb. Let's go through each of the 5 S's:

1. Swaddle

Newborn babies have what's called a Moro reflex, or startle reflex, which makes them jerk suddenly. A swaddle will prevent them from waking up and give them a sense of security and comfort. It's almost like a gentle hug.

It's not uncommon for moms to think their baby doesn't like to be swaddled, but I encourage them to keep trying a little bit longer. Some babies may not like the process of getting into their swaddle, but they almost always sleep for longer stretches once they're swaddled.

It's also important to make sure you're swaddling them correctly. You want their arms to be snug and straight by their side, with their hips loose and flexed. Stop swaddling once your baby starts to roll over, which can be as early as 2 months.

2. Side or stomach

While all babies should sleep on their backs, they often like to be held on their sides or on their stomachs. Having gentle pressure on their sides or stomachs keeps them calm and relaxed. You can lie them on their side in their crib while you are settling them, or pick them up and set them over your shoulder or across your forearm with your hand supporting their head. These are most likely the positions they were in while they were in the womb.

3. Shhh

When trying to calm your baby, make a "shhh" sound or play white noise. This mimics the sound of blood flowing in the womb, which is louder than a vacuum when they're inside you. Contrary to popular belief, babies actually prefer a noisy environment when sleeping, so you don't need to tip-toe around a sleeping baby at this stage: they're used to a lot of noise.

4. Swing

Babies love movement! Try swinging or moving up and down in fast, tiny movements while supporting your baby's head and neck. You can also rock back and forth with a slight bend in the knees or bounce on a yoga ball. You will quickly learn what type of movement your baby likes best.

5. Suck

Sucking lowers a baby's heart rate, blood pressure, and stress levels. Pacifiers are great for this during the night, and pacifier use at bedtime has been linked to a lower risk of SIDS.[8] If you're breastfeeding your baby, wait until it's well-established before introducing a pacifier. In the meantime, you can use your finger.

The 5 S's are a great way to calm and comfort your little one, and they do work if done properly and in the right order, as they're listed above. You don't have to feel like you're the only one who can settle your baby, either. Your partner can too!

We learn by doing, so first try giving your baby to your partner, telling them what to do, and then leaving them alone. Give them at least 45 minutes to figure it out together. I know it can be tempting to jump in, especially if you hear your baby crying and know you can soothe them quickly, but it's important for all partners to learn how to soothe their baby as well. If you can't stop yourself from butting in, leave the house and allow them to keep trying.

You might be wondering, once the baby is asleep, what do you do when it's time for a feed? Unless your pediatrician has advised waking them for frequent feeding due to low weight gain, I think it's always best to let them sleep. Trust their cues: babies will wake when they need food. Don't disturb the baby or interact with them unless necessary, and remember that you typically only need to change their diaper in the middle of the night if it's dirty.

What to Expect: Birth to 8 Weeks

Newborn babies tend to be noisy sleepers. The saying "sleep like a baby" implies that babies sleep peacefully, but this isn't typically the case. It is also common for newborns to wake up frequently and fuss a little, which often escalates to crying.

Some babies will sleep for long stints, while others will stay awake for long periods and take short naps. Babies don't need to consolidate their sleep in 8 hours at night. If you wake up 6 times during the night, you'll be exhausted even though you have slept for a reasonable amount of time overall. Babies can wake up 6 times, go back to sleep, and still wake up refreshed. As parents, we lose sleep during the newborn phase, but your baby isn't suffering one bit.

From birth to 8 weeks, or until they develop a circadian rhythm, all of their sleep will be a series of naps. These naps can last anywhere from 30 minutes to 4 hours. Newborns will wake up more at certain times of the day than others and at nighttime, they likely won't sleep for longer than 2-3 hours.

Their biological sleep rhythms won't develop until 8-12 weeks, so they don't yet know the difference between the day and night. A common term is "reverse cycle," and many parents tend to think their baby has the day and night mixed up, but in reality, they don't know the difference yet. Your milk-making hormones are highest at night, which is why babies want to be awake at night to feed. Don't try to keep them up during the day, hoping they will sleep better at night. It will only make things worse.

With babies less than 8 weeks old, it's important to create a good sleeping environment. You can do this by:

- Playing white noise, soft music, a nature recording, a fan, or a gurgling aquarium. These sounds will muffle other noises and soothe your baby.

- Using blackout curtains: darkness causes the pineal gland to produce and release melatonin
- Keeping the room between 62-68°F (16-20°C)

Since your baby spent the past 9 months being with you all the time, it's normal for them to want to be near you all the time. However, they need to become familiar with the crib or bassinet and get used to being in it consistently if this is where you want them to sleep. Starting when you come home from the hospital, try to do at least 2 naps a day in the crib. It should be in the same spot all the time, and ideally, somewhere close to you.

Survive the Phase

You're going to be tired in those early newborn days. Sometimes you're going to have to do whatever it takes to survive. Here are some tips to make the first 8 weeks easier:

Prevent Your Baby From Being Overtired and Avoid Overstimulation

Don't let your baby stay awake too long, and try to minimize crying. If your baby gets overtired, the stress hormone, cortisol, kicks in and it becomes harder for them to relax and sleep.

At this point, they will need extra soothing and attention to get them to sleep. Some babies may not give sleep cues until they are already overtired, so keep an eye on the clock. Newborns stay awake for 2 hours max, with most newborns not staying awake for longer than 30-90 minutes.

It is also important to be aware of overstimulation. All the new sounds and things to look at can be very exciting and stimulating for a newborn. Your baby will get overtired faster if they're in a new environment with lots of new things around them.

Do What Works

It takes 8-12 weeks for babies to develop a circadian rhythm, so do whatever you need to do to help your baby sleep.[9] There's no reason to be stingy with soothing: you're not going to create bad habits or spoil your baby.

Don't get too caught up in all the dogma about newborn sleep. Use whatever tools you have as long as they are safe and your baby is sleeping in a safe place at all times. These are the most common myths I hear:

1. Prevent junk sleep

Junk sleep is considered any daytime sleep that isn't in a crib, and it's normally looked down upon. However, the truth is that many babies will sleep far longer and more deeply on their parent or while moving. Don't feel like you have to lie your baby down for every nap. Throughout history, babies have slept wherever their mom was and sometimes even on top of her.

2. Avoid contact naps

A contact nap is when your baby sleeps on you. Newborns love to be close to their mothers, and they typically are at their calmest on their mother's chest. If your baby won't sleep without you holding them at first, that's okay. There are safe ways to do this, such as:

- Using a sling or carrier
- Sleeping with baby and mom tummy to tummy. Make sure you are lightly dressed (no sweaters), lying at an angle in bed (make a backrest out of pillows) so the baby's head is higher than their bottom, and all pillows and blankets are away from the baby.

3. Never feed a baby to sleep

Feeding babies to sleep is the biological norm, and it's been happening for centuries. Breast milk in the evening contains higher levels of melatonin and helps your baby fall asleep. The sucking reflex also releases the hormone cholecystokinin (CCK), resulting in a very sleepy feeling. Feeding your baby soothes them quickly and is extremely comforting, but moms often feel guilty for feeding their babies to sleep.[10] If you're doing it and it's working for you, keep going! If it's not working, change things up.

4. Always put your baby down drowsy but awake

The idea of drowsy but awake seems to be the holy grail of teaching your baby to sleep on their own. This works great for some parents, but some babies are awake and then asleep without that transition period. Often, parents feel like they're failing when their baby needs a little help to go to sleep, but this is okay and perfectly normal.

Plan For Nighttime

Nighttime can be extremely challenging with a newborn but with some preparation, you can make things easier.

First, it is important to be aware of the witching hour. This is the time when an otherwise content baby is extremely fussy and can't be settled. For most babies, it occurs between 5:00 p.m. and 11:00 p.m. It can last from a few minutes to a couple of hours, and for most babies, it starts to occur between 2-3 weeks, peaking at 6 weeks after birth.

To survive this time, use whatever tools you need to settle your baby. If you know it's coming, it will be easier to have an attitude of "let's buckle up and do this!" instead of stressing.

During this phase, plan to be awake during the night. It is okay if you do not sleep in the same bed, or at the same time, as your partner. It's best to divide and conquer. Mom might go to bed at 9 p.m. and get up at 1 a.m., and then go back to sleep until 3 a.m. and get up again at 6 a.m. Your partner might go to bed at midnight and wake up at 7 a.m. The key is being strategic so everyone gets some sleep.

It is also important to set yourself up for success. Having a bedside kit can be a great way to prepare for those long nights. Your kit might include:

- Water bottle with a straw (you'll get very thirsty when you start breastfeeding)
- Snacks: you might get hungry or need to eat to take pain medication
- Any medication you may need
- Diapers, wipes, and a hand towel so you can quickly change your baby in bed between your legs without getting up
- Burp cloth
- Extra baby clothes
- Breast pads

- Saline nasal spray: when your baby is congested, this will help open their airway so they can breathe while they're on the breast
- Lip balm

Lastly, use a mattress protector on the baby's mattress. Some people have a mattress protector, then a fitted sheet, then another protector, then another fitted sheet. This way, if a diaper leaks or your baby spits up, you can take off the top 2 layers and have fresh sheets, and you'll get back to bed sooner.

It Won't Last Forever

Like every season in parenting, this one won't last forever. You don't have to love every moment, but remember that they will pass.

Although it can be difficult, it's best to accept that your baby is not going to have a sleep schedule at first, and you need to follow their lead. Be present and relaxed, and know that each time you respond to your baby's cries, you are creating the conditions for healthy relationships, emotional regulation, and a balanced brain.

Babies can sense how we feel, and this will affect their feelings too. If you're tense and feeling frustrated, your baby will sense that and not feel comfortable going to sleep. Do what you need to do to help yourself calm down and relax before trying to calm your baby.

Remember, crying and fussiness are normally at their worst at around 6 weeks, but then they gradually improve. After this period, the baby starts to cry less, sleep longer, and need less settling. Sleep is normally the best at around 8 weeks, so hang in there!

What to Expect: 8 Weeks-4 Months

As you enter the next postpartum phase, your newborn's sleep will become a bit more structured. You can tell you've hit this milestone when your baby looks at you and smiles as they acknowledge your presence. Seeing the love your little one has for you makes the challenges of the past 8 weeks worth it!

By this point, nighttime feeds may reduce to 1-3 per night and your baby will likely sleep for longer stretches, typically 3-6 hours at a time. It's important to pay attention to their sleep environment as their sleep patterns change. As their circadian rhythm starts to develop, lighting becomes more critical. The circadian rhythm is your natural body clock that tells you when it's time to wake and sleep, and it is affected by sunlight.

To help with their sleep rhythms, it's important to expose the baby to lots of natural light during the day. You can open the windows or spend some time outside in the shade. Keep your baby out of direct sunlight until they are 6 months old.[11]

When your baby is napping during the day, dim the room, and avoid turning lights on at night. Humans sleep best in dark, cool, quiet places. When the sun goes down, use red light or dim nightlights if you need a light to see. Lights from electronics will interfere with your baby's circadian rhythm, so put your phone or tablet away while you're putting your baby to sleep.

You can continue to use white noise to drown out any sounds, and you might notice your baby is more sensitive to loud environments than before. Be aware of how your baby's sleep environment has changed by this point. Have the seasons changed? Is it warmer or colder, or is there light earlier in the morning? All these changes will affect your baby's sleep patterns, so be sure to adjust clothing and their environment accordingly.

It's still too early for your baby to have a daytime routine, but you can start working on a nighttime routine. Even if it's not consistent every night, having a routine will help your baby relax and promote a more consistent sleep pattern.

One way to do this is to start implementing a specific bedtime routine. This might look like having a bath before bed, putting on PJs, reading a story, feeding, swaddling, and then being put to bed with a kiss. To establish a bedtime routine, keep it consistent every time you put your baby to bed. It also helps to have a word or phrase you say to your baby when you put them to bed, such as "Shh, it's sleep time, night night."

This consistent routine cues your baby that it's time to go to sleep. You'll also want to pick a consistent bedtime between 6-8 p.m. The best bedtime for your baby will vary, but keep in mind that the baby will need 11-13 hours of sleep each night.

When your baby gets older, naps will become part of a daily routine, but for now, naps will be very unpredictable since newborns tend to nap on demand. They will wake up at different times and nap for different lengths of time. This is okay! Don't worry too much about a schedule, and go with the flow. Your baby will likely continue to want to be held and have contact naps a lot of the time, and that's okay too!

Try to focus on at least 1-2 good naps each day. A good nap is at least 1 hour long. Other naps throughout the day may be shorter. Having naps every 1-2 hours is an important part of getting longer periods of sleep at night.

It may be frustrating if your baby won't nap without sucking on mom's nipple or a bottle nipple. To help them nap without being latched, try gently breaking the seal and putting slight pressure under their chin so their mouth closes and their tongue presses against the roof of their mouth. A lot of the time, they'll start sucking on the top of their mouth instead.

What to Expect: 4-6 Months

Can you believe it? Your little one is already 4 months old! At this point, bedtime should still be between 6 and 8 p.m. If it's later, move it back 15 minutes each night. Your baby will also start to have more scheduled naps – typically, around 3 per day.

Sleep Regression

It's also common for your baby to have sleep regression around this time, and a previously good sleeper might suddenly end up with very broken rest.

Although this is challenging to deal with, know that you're not alone! This is called the 4-month sleep regression, although it can happen at any age, including 4 months, 6 months, 8 months, 12 months, or even 2 years.

You'll recognize it because out of the blue, your baby will go from sleeping really well or fairly well to being up at all hours, wanting to be soothed or fed. They may be constantly cranky at night. They will typically sleep less, be extra fussy, have trouble falling asleep, resist naps, and be hungrier at night. This might be a scary thought, but the reality is, there's no way to prevent sleep regression. It's a normal part of development, which means your baby is growing!

Some of the possible causes of sleep regression are:

- Growth spurt: it might happen when your baby is reaching a developmental milestone. Dutch researchers Vanderijt and Plooij published a book, *The Wonder Weeks,* and according to their research, growth spurts occur at weeks 5, 8, 12, 19, 26, 37, 46, and 55.[12]
- Disruption in routine: this might include traveling or having a new babysitter. Once your baby gets used to

their routine, you'll notice how little changes can quickly impact their sleep patterns.
- Illness: feeling unwell will usually impact your child's sleep and may make them restless and fussy.

It's not easy to deal with your baby's sleep regression, but baby sleep patterns change all the time. Most sleep regressions last 2 to 6 weeks and your baby's sleep patterns then return to normal.

Adjust your schedule to work around their fussiness and give them more cuddle time. If you have someone to help you, whether it's your partner or another support person, tag team it! When your baby isn't sleeping well, bedtime can be exhausting, so don't be afraid to ask for help.

Try to view this as extra time you get to spend with your baby, as this may help you feel more positive when nothing you are doing gets them to sleep and you've had barely any sleep yourself for the past few days or weeks.

It's also important to remember that they're not bad sleepers; they're just having a hard time. Keep their routine normal during the regression, especially at bedtime. This will help to keep them calm and encourage them to return to their previous sleeping patterns.

You should remember to get your baby to bed before they're overtired, and make sure they get enough sleep during the day. Babies who don't will struggle more to sleep at night.

Is Sleep Training Necessary?

When you become a mom, it likely won't be long before someone asks you how your baby is sleeping. As a society, we're obsessed with babies "sleeping through the night," and this can be really damaging for new moms. It can cause a lot of guilt and concern, since sleep-deprived moms start to think there's something wrong with their babies or that they're doing something wrong.

Good sleeping habits are generally thought to include a consistent bedtime, independently falling asleep, and sleeping in a crib. Some parents successfully sleep train their babies at 3 months, but 4-6 months is usually when sleep experts recommend you start sleep training. They believe your baby is physically and emotionally ready to sleep through the night around this time.

You don't need to look very far to find dozens of different sleep training methods that guarantee they'll get your baby sleeping through the night. Although they do work for some parents, the truth is, babies don't sleep like adults. They lack hormonal regulators, and their sleep cycle is about half the length of an adult's sleep cycle.[13] This means they typically wake up twice as much as you do during the night, moving into a light sleep state approximately every 25 minutes. Because they want to be near you, they start crying when they wake up. Remember that they aren't doing this to manipulate you.

They are crying because a need is not being met and it's the only way they can communicate. The unfulfilled need could be hunger, dirty diapers, feeling unwell, or being scared or lonely. Babies need human interaction and physical contact, and being held is a need, not a want.

It's easy to feel like a failure when sleep training isn't working for you, but in reality, it's not wired into your baby's DNA to sleep alone or sleep through the night. If you choose to follow the no-cry sleep method and go to your baby whenever they cry so you can rock, hold, hug, feed, give them a pacific, etc., that is okay.

If you do nothing to change your baby's sleep patterns, they will sleep independently when they are ready and no longer need you. Some parents think their baby will not develop normally and will have behavioral or sleep issues their whole lives if they don't sleep train them, but this is simply not true. Sleep training is an option, not a necessity. The truth is, whether your child is a good sleeper or not has to do more with temperament than training.[14]

The bottom line is we tend to have unrealistic sleep expectations for babies. Your sleep journey with your baby will not be linear; there will be ups and downs throughout the entire process. Most children don't sleep through the night until they are over 2 years old, although this doesn't mean they will be waking every hour until then.

Sleep training works for some families, but it's not mandatory. Like most parenting decisions, you should decide what works for you and your baby.

Self-Soothing – The Baby Sleep Industry's Favorite Word

Another idea you will hear frequently is that you need to teach your baby how to "self-soothe." Self-soothing is the process of babies calming and settling themselves to sleep. In other words, they develop the ability to regulate their own emotions and fall asleep without you.

The problem is that babies can't self-regulate their emotions, since their brains aren't developed enough. The ability to self-soothe depends on the neocortex of the brain, which is the place that allows us to rationalize, analyze, and mediate our responses.

This is actually one of the last parts of your brain to mature, which is why young children rely on you to help them regulate their emotions until they're capable of doing it themselves.[15]

Self-soothing is physically impossible at this age, but what is possible is compliance and dissociation. If you don't come when your baby cries, they will learn to stop crying because they have learned that nothing happens when they cry. It doesn't mean your baby is necessarily sleeping through the night and it doesn't mean they're peaceful.[16]

In many cases, it also trains children that their needs don't matter. If we repeatedly ignore our babies, they'll believe they're not worthy of attention, comfort, and affection. Although you may be sold on the idea that your baby is learning to self-soothe, sleep training merely silences your baby.[17]

Learning to self-soothe doesn't happen over the course of a few nights while letting your baby cry it out. It's something that happens over time as a baby learns to control and process emotions such as fear and loneliness. It happens as they develop a secure bond with their caregivers, helping them to realize their environment is safe.[18]

When you respond to your baby's cry, you're telling them:

- You are safe
- You are loved
- You can turn to me for help
- You are not alone
- You can trust me

Babies' brains develop fully when their needs are responded to. Research suggests that extinction methods, such as cry it out, may result in better sleep in the short-term, but all babies have similar sleep patterns around 1 year old, regardless of the sleep training method their parents used. The conclusion is that sleep training methods that involve crying aren't necessary in the long-term.[19]

There are many ways other than sleep training to encourage babies to sleep.

- Be consistent: quickly answering your newborn's cries and creating a calm, soothing environment can encourage your baby to fall asleep swiftly. They'll be reassured that you're ready to answer their needs at any time, and so will require less support to settle and will stay settled for longer. In time, your baby will mature and become less dependent on you. Every child develops at their own pace, so there's no set time when this occurs.

• Experiment with different soothing techniques: try different strategies, but bear in mind that what works at one time may not work in the future. Be open to trying new techniques and use them as needed.

• Let them win: you want your baby to fall asleep independently, and they want to be held. This can start to feel like a fight. Take the pressure off your shoulders and remember that babies don't need to fall asleep independently in order to sleep through the night. If your baby needs to be rocked, held, or nursed to go to sleep, that's okay. It doesn't mean they'll never sleep without your help.

Using the no-cry method and responding to your baby's cries throughout the night is really challenging at times. Although you are reassuring your baby that their needs matter, it is still extremely exhausting, so hang in there.

If you are having real problems, you might want to consider talking to a sleep coach. However, first, you should focus on providing:

- A peaceful environment, which is the right temperature, not too dark or too light, white noise, and no blue light
- A consistent bedtime routine, including time for connection and time to wind down
- Some natural light every day

You should also consider whether they are:

- Having too many or too few naps
- Having naps too close to bedtime
- Going through a developmental milestone that is disrupting their sleep

You should also look for red flags where a sleep coach would be helpful, such as:

- Snoring, mouth breathing, or any other obvious discomfort while sleeping
- Having feeding issues (latching, tongue-tie, not getting enough milk) along with trouble sleeping

7
Newborn Care 101

Taking care of a newborn is often very complicated, and since babies don't come with a manual, this chapter will cover everything you need to know about caring for your baby.

Let's talk about safety first.

Safety

The first thing to know about newborn safety is that you should never leave your baby alone on a changing table, bed, sofa, or chair. When you're not able to hold your baby, put them in a safe place, such as a crib or a playpen. It might seem silly, since newborns don't yet have the ability to crawl or stand, but they can still wriggle and end up in unsafe positions. No matter the age of your baby, you should avoid leaving them alone in an unsafe place.

By 3 months old, your baby will start to squirm and can easily fall off surfaces. They may even be rolling over at this point. They're also starting to grasp objects, so keep a close eye on any hazardous objects they can reach.

When it comes to safety measures, a properly installed car seat is one of the most important ways to keep your baby safe. Your baby should always be in regular clothes when they're in their car seat, and thick outwear should not be worn. Chest clips should be level with your baby's armpits, right over their sternum. When you push on the car seat, it shouldn't move more than an inch in either direction.[1] If anyone other than yourself or your partner will be putting your baby in their seat, make sure they're aware of these guidelines as well.

Lifting and Carrying Your Baby

A newborn baby needs support, especially for their head and neck. The head makes up about a third of their body weight, and the neck muscles aren't developed enough to support and control that much weight yet.[2] This is also why you should never throw your baby up in the air.

When you are holding your baby, use the following positions

Shoulder Hold

Belly Hold

Cradle Hold

Lap Hold

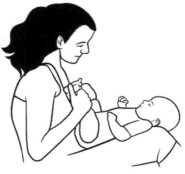

When putting your newborn down, use one hand to support their bottom and the other hand stretched wide around the back of their head and neck. Release the hand on their bottom first and then release the other hand from their head. To pick up your newborn, do the same method in reverse. Never lift your newborn by or under their arms.

Every time you put them down, alternate which way their head is turned and also which end of the crib you put their head on. This is because plagiocephaly or "flattened head shape" is an extremely common condition in babies that is usually preventable as long as you constantly alternate.[3]

Soft Spot (Fontanelles)

When it comes to newborn safety, be aware of their soft spots. There are two parts of your newborn's skull that haven't closed yet, known as the soft spots or fontanelles. The larger one is on the top of the head, and the smaller one is on the back of the head.

The top one closes between 12-18 months of age and the back one closes between 2-3 months of age. It's safe to touch them gently because they're covered by a thick membrane, but be sure to protect them from bumping into any hard or sharp objects.[4]

Baby-Wearing

In the early days, it's normal for your baby to want to be close to you nearly all of the time. Baby-wearing is a great way to bond with your baby, while keeping your hands free. Newborns can be worn right away as long as they are at least 8 pounds and don't have any specific medical conditions.[5]

Aside from letting you use both hands, baby-wearing has many benefits, including:

- Helps create a strong maternal bond
- Fosters cue-based feeding
- Allows them to observe new environments
- Makes your baby feel calm, safe, and loved
- Often makes them sleepy
- Allows bonding time for your partner

There are numerous types of carriers out there, such as structured carriers, slings, and wraps. It may be helpful to test out a few and see which one you and your baby are happiest in.

Safe baby-wearing is crucial, especially in the newborn stage, and it includes proper positioning of your baby.

For the first 6 months, it's recommended that you carry your infant facing towards you. To prevent hip dysplasia, you want your baby's legs to make an "M" shape around your tummy, instead dangling straight down.[6]

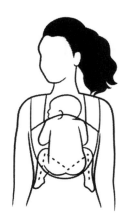

There are a few things you need to look out for while baby-wearing. To help you remember, check the TICKS:

T: Tight – your baby is secure and close to you
I: In view at all times – your baby is visible to you at a glance
C: Close enough to kiss – their head is just below your chin
K: Keep chin off chest – your baby's chin needs to be raised and not tucked down. Their head should be slightly lifted backwards so they have a clear airway
S: Support the back – your baby's back is in a natural, straight position, not curled forward[7]

You also want to keep temperature in mind when baby-wearing. If you're somewhere warm, the insert of your baby carrier may get too hot when combined with your body heat.

Umbilical Cord Care

Many people don't know that a newborn's umbilical cord will need proper care after the birth. The cord will be cut shortly after your baby is born, but the stump will remain until it falls off on its own, between 10 days and 3 weeks after the birth.

The stump will change from yellow to brown, and then to black. You'll generally want to leave the area alone, but expose the stump to air to help it dry out. Until it falls off, keep the front of your baby's diaper folded down to avoid covering the stump. Never submerge their navel in water until it has fallen off and healed. Only give your baby a sponge bath until then, since this is the best way to keep the stump nice and dry. An unpleasant smell and small amounts of clear or yellow watery fluid coming from your baby's navel are both normal.

See a doctor if: the naval area looks red, or has a foul odor with discharge.[8]

Penis Care

If you have a baby boy, be sure to clean the genital area daily with warm water. During cleaning and diaper changes, erections are also normal, so don't be afraid to clean the penis and scrotum area well.

Uncircumcised Care

If they're uncircumcised, don't attempt to retract the foreskin and clean it. Spontaneous erections will help break the adhesion and once your son gains control of his hands, he will pull it around and sort out the stretching on his own terms. Full retraction of the foreskin may not occur until around age 7.

See a doctor if: There's excessive redness or discharge from the penis.[9]

Circumcision Care

After circumcision, doctors will normally cover the tip with gauze and petroleum jelly. After each diaper change, wipe the tip clean with warm water and continue to apply petroleum jelly so the tip doesn't stick to the diaper. Redness and irritation are normal for the first few days.

Once the circumcision heals, it is important to push on the pubic fat pad around the penis to expose the tip and clean around it with each diaper change. This will ensure that the penis is not retracted into the fat pad for long periods, and prevent adhesion.

See a doctor if: there's redness or swelling after the first few days, or pus-filled blisters form.[10]

Vagina Care

If you have a baby girl, always wipe from front to back during diaper changes and when cleaning. Gently do a thorough

Jocelyn Goodwin

cleaning between all the creases. Thick, milky discharge in the vagina is normal and doesn't need to be cleaned away.[11]

Diapers and Creams

No matter how tiny they may be, newborn babies will still use a lot of diapers. The first thing you need to know is how to tell when their diaper is wet or dirty.

Before they poop, most babies will grunt and grimace, but if they don't, you might have to use your sense of smell. If you're using modern disposable diapers, they often come with color-changing stripes that turn from yellow to blue to indicate that the diaper is wet.

Whether you use disposable or cloth diapers, I recommend setting up a diaper changing area to make it easier for yourself. This area should be somewhere that is easily accessible and has a flat surface. It doesn't necessarily need to be a changing table. At night, you can do diaper changes in bed if you want, and this can really maximize sleep time.

Make sure your diaper changing area has:

- Clean diapers (not all diapers are created equal, so try a variety of brands)
- Fasteners if you're using cloth diapers
- Diaper ointment
- Pre-moistened wipes or a washcloth and warm water (for a newborn, you can use a cotton ball and warm water)
- An extra change of clothes
- A diaper pail (if you're not using a diaper pail, you'll want to take out the trash every day to avoid the smell)

Although changing a diaper may seem simple, your baby might not always want to cooperate. Here are the steps for a relatively peaceful diaper change:

1. Use gentle touches and talk softly
2. Lay your baby on their back
3. Remove their dirty diaper swiftly and roll it up. Every second counts with anything smelly!
4. Gently wipe the genital area and make sure you get all the creases
5. Wash your hands while your baby's bum airs out or pat it dry with a paper towel if needed. It's important for their bottom to be dry before applying diaper ointment or a diaper
6. Apply diaper rash cream or ointment to any affected areas, as this can be a great way to prevent diaper rash
7. Raise your baby's legs and lower body by their ankles and slide a clean diaper underneath
8. Pull the front part of the diaper up between your baby's legs and lay it on their belly. Next, lift the wings on the left and right to the front of the diaper. Each wing should be symmetrical on the baby's tummy. You should be able to comfortably run 2 fingers between the diaper and their stomach. Every diaper brand is different, but the process is generally the same
9. Turn the leg cuffs out to prevent leaks

Warning! Exposure to air may make baby boys urinate. Your boy might surprise you with a fountain of pee midway through a diaper change. It's helpful to keep the penis covered with a dry cloth when he is undressed and make sure his penis is pointing downwards when you put the new diaper on.

Clothing

Buying clothing for your newborn baby is one of the most fun parts of preparing to be a new mom! However, there's a safety aspect to the clothing they wear.

We mentioned earlier that you should choose natural fibers for breathability and temperature regulation. You'll also want the material to be soft.

For weeks 0-2, kimonos can be great for babies to wear. They wrap around your baby's body and snap on the side. They're less likely to rub and irritate the umbilical cord stump and you don't have to pull them over your baby's head. Even if you choose other clothing styles, you should avoid putting pants on your baby until their umbilical cord stump heals.

For week 2 and beyond, a onesie and a footed sleeper work almost all of the time. Clothes with zippers tend to be the easiest. If it doesn't have zippers, try something with snaps, although this will certainly be more time-consuming and frustrating in the middle of the night. Avoid buttons, as they take too much time to fasten and you'll regret it around 2 a.m. when you're having to re-button your baby in the dark.

No matter what clothing you put your baby in, it's important that it fits properly. You don't want it to be too big because it could ride up and block their ability to breathe. On the other hand, you don't want it to be too tight because it will be uncomfortable and increase their likely hood of getting diaper rash.

Socks and shoes are only needed for warmth during this phase, and they rarely stay on anyway. If it's cold, stick to footed outfits.

Temperature

When you're dressing your newborn, temperature is always a factor. You'll want to have options for both cold and warm days.

You can use your own body temperature to gauge how you should dress your infant.

When you're going out of the house, many people adhere to the "what you're wearing plus 1 layer" rule. Layers are always going to be best since you can easily add or remove them if necessary.

Think about your climate when dressing your baby or purchasing clothes for them. If you live in a cold climate, your baby should be covered from head to toe when going outside, including a hat, mittens, socks, and a blanket. A bunting bag or sleeping bag may also be ideal! These are essentially thick blankets that fit over a stroller. When you go back indoors, make sure you remove extra layers promptly to avoid overheating.

If you live in a hot climate and the weather is over 75°F, dress your baby in a single layer of clothing, a lightweight hat, and possibly sunglasses. It is also beneficial to have a light blanket for sun protection.

Although you may have the best intentions, it's very easy to overdress a baby. Babies sweat less and generate more heat than adults, so they are at a higher risk of overheating. To avoid this, don't put hats or mittens on your baby at home. It's normal for a newborn's hands and feet to be slightly purple and cold. To tell whether your baby is hot or cold, feel the skin on their tummy, above the breast bone, or on their upper back.

At night time, room temperature should be between 68 and 72°F (20-22°C). You can put your baby in a swaddle or a wearable blanket (depending on their age and ability to roll over). The AAP recommends that babies don't sleep in a hat, to avoid overheating.[12]

Bathing Your Little One

Bath time will eventually become a fun time with your baby, but it can be intimidating at first. Until their umbilical cord falls off, you're only going to give them sponge baths. How to give a newborn a sponge bath is covered in Chapter 3.

Newborns really only need 2-3 proper baths a week, and any more than that will dry their skin out. A baby's skin is fragile and more sensitive than an adult's, so it is important to use gentle products that are specially formulated for newborns.

When giving your baby a bath, never leave them alone for any amount of time. If you need to leave for some reason, wrap them in a towel and take them with you.

Your baby's first few baths should be short. If they get upset, go back to sponge baths and then slowly introduce the tub again.

To give your newborn a tub bath, here are the steps:

1. Use an infant tub or 2-3 inches of warm water at the bottom of a tub or sink
2. Always test the water with the inside of your wrist to make sure it's not too hot. The temperature should be around 100°F or 38°C[13]
3. Place the baby in the bath, feet first
4. Wash the baby's face with plain water
5. Add a small amount of soap to a washcloth and gently wipe their body from top to bottom, and then rinse
6. Gently tilt the baby's head back and pour water over their head, avoiding their eyes
7. Add a small amount of shampoo and gently rub their hair
8. Rinse with water and use a soft baby hairbrush on their scalp (this can be used over the soft spot as well)
9. Dry their body thoroughly and apply lotion. This is important because newborn skin is more prone to

dryness and potential irritation, since it's thinner than adult skin

10. Once your baby is completely dry, put on their diaper and clothes

Cleaning Your Baby's Ears, Eyes, and Nose

Even though your baby isn't moving around a ton yet, you might be surprised how dirty their ears, eyes, and nose can get. On days you aren't giving them a bath, wipe these three areas down. Using a cotton ball and warm water will do the trick.

For their eyes, wipe from the inside to outside corner, and use a new cotton ball for each eye. For the nose, gently wipe around each nostril to get rid of any dried or liquid mucus. Wipe around the ears, but leave the earwax alone, as it's protecting their ears and blocking any germs that might cause infection. Never stick anything in your baby's ears, since this can damage them.

Taking Care of Your Baby's Nails

Your baby will have fingernails from the day they're born, and they might even be long right after they're born. In the newborn phase, you may cover your baby's hands with baby mittens or socks to prevent them from scratching their face or you, but be careful of overheating if it's hot out.

You can also cut their nails, but this may actually feel like the scariest thing since birth! If you decide to cut their nails, purchase baby nail clippers and do it when they're calm, or even when they're sleeping. If this seems too scary, you can start by filing their nails down gradually so they are not as sharp.

You might also notice that your newborn's toes overlap, and sometimes their nails may look ingrown. This is very normal.

Hunger Cues

You're probably already aware that babies don't have "mealtimes" like older children and adults, so you don't need to schedule feeding times; you need to feed your baby when they are hungry. That might leave you wondering how you'll know when they're ready to eat.

A lot of us think that crying is a good hunger cue, but most people fail to realize that babies tend to give a whole slew of other cues first. Crying is often the last resort, and waiting until your baby cries might not be the best idea.

Ideally, you should be looking out for early hunger cues. Some of the most common include:

- Smacking or licking the lips
- Sucking on various parts of the body, including lips, toes, hands, and fingers.
- Sticking the tongue out of the mouth
- Opening and closing the mouth

As time passes, if your baby hasn't received any food to satisfy their hunger, they might begin to give "active" hunger cues. Some of these active cues include:

- Pulling on your clothes in an attempt to get into a feeding position
- Turning their head towards your chest
- Fussing or breathing too fast
- Moving the arms and legs about more than usual
- Showing discomfort through grunts and whining sounds
- Fidgeting about or squirming around
- Hitting your arm and chest repeatedly
- Smiling and cooing

Finally, your baby might give some "late" hunger cues, including crying. A hunger cry is usually different from other types of crying in pitch and length. It's normally short, low, and typically rises and falls repeatedly. Another late hunger cue your baby might give you is moving the head from side to side in a frantic manner.[14]

It's important to remember that hunger cues change based on age as well.

From 0-4 months, your baby may show hunger by:

- Waking up and tossing themselves around
- Seeming restless
- Crying or fussing
- Sucking on their fist
- Opening their mouth
- Making sucking noises and motions
- Rooting around on the chest of whoever is holding them

Babies between 4 and 6 months may show hunger by:

- Gazing at the caregiver
- Crying or fussing
- Moving the head toward the breast or bottle
- Smiling or cooing during the feeding session to indicate they want more[15]

How Often and How Long Should I Feed My Baby?

When deciding how often you should feed your newborn baby, be guided by their hunger cues and satiety cues.

Whether you're bottle-feeding or breastfeeding, don't compare your baby to other babies. Some babies will prefer to snack all day with small, short feeds, and some will prefer larger feeds. It's possible for bigger babies to want more milk and smaller babies to want less milk, and vice versa. Trust your baby's instincts.

You will see these differences most often in breastfed babies. Some will take a full feed in 10 minutes, while others take 40 minutes to get the same amount. One baby might stay for 30 minutes on each breast, while another baby might stay for only 15 minutes on only one breast. For each baby and mom, the suck is different, the production is different, and the flow is different. If you let breastfed babies control how often and how long they feed, they will, on average, consume the right amount of milk for their body weight across their various meals.

Bottle-fed babies will typically go longer between feeds because formula takes longer to digest, but for breastfed babies, it's normal to feel like your baby wants to eat all the time. Although this is hard work, don't worry about feeding your baby too often: it's impossible to breastfeed too much because your baby is signaling to your milk-making hormones how much they need to produce to support your baby. Over time, your supply will catch up and your baby will get more efficient at feeding, and feed less often.

If you're one of the lucky moms whose baby sleeps through the night at 8 weeks old, you don't need to worry about waking them up to feed them, as long as they're gaining weight and you have a good milk supply. If your supply starts to weaken or their weight drops, wake your baby around every 3-4 hours for a feed.

Cluster Feeding

Cluster feeding is when your baby wants to feed even more frequently, sometimes consistently, and it can happen at any time. This behavior is typically only seen in breastfed babies, but it can occur in formula-fed babies when they are going through a growth spurt.

For breastfeeding moms, when your baby is cluster feeding, it might feel like they never leave your breast, and they're unsatisfied no matter how much they eat. This behavior doesn't happen all day, but typically for a chunk of time in a day. However, it can still be exhausting for a breastfeeding mom. Give some time for your supply to catch up with the demand and the cluster feeding should slow down.

How to Know if Your Baby Is Getting Enough Milk

This is normally a question only breastfeeding moms ask, but it's important to look for signs instead of counting ounces for formula-fed babies as well. Our society is obsessed with numbers! Make sure you also trust nature and your baby's instincts. Pay attention to the numbers, but don't be surprised if they don't line up exactly with what your baby seems to need.

Moms often find reassurance in expressing milk or formula feeding because then they know exactly how much their baby is consuming, but if you let a breastfed baby feed when they want and for as long as they want, they will consume everything they need. This is one of the beauties of breastfeeding.

Whether you're breastfeeding or formula-feeding, look for the signs on the following chart.[16]

WELL-FED	NOT WELL-FED
Soft, relaxed, and open hands	Splotchy hands and tightly closed fists
6 wet diapers per day	Less than 6 wet diapers per day
Wet tears when crying	Tearless crying
Soft lips	Cracked lips or dry mouth
Skin bounces back when gently pressed	Skin is dry and slack
Vibrant eyes	Sunken eyes
Engaged	Lack of concertration
Lots of expressions	No emotions or enthusiasm
Easy to settle	Unusually sleepy
Alert and active	Poop is extremely hard and difficult to pass
Poop is soft	Sunken "soft spot" on top of the head
Hitting milestones	Falling asleep after just 2 sucks when feeding
Hearing your baby swallow while feeding	Not sleeping, or waking frequently and showing signs of anger
Baby gets drowsy after feeding	Less than 8 feeds in 24 hours

It can be helpful to track everything for the first 2-4 weeks until your baby's weight surpasses their birth weight or you feel confident about their eating. You can also track their sleep, number of feeds, and length of feeds, so you have data to share with your doctor if you think there's a problem.

Note: If your baby is under 6 months old, they only need to drink breast milk or infant formula. There's no need for water for hydration.

Number of Pees and Poops

Despite their small size, newborns use a lot of diapers. Your newborn should have 6-10 wet diapers per day.[17] As for soiled diapers, there is a large range of what's considered normal. Newborns may poop as frequently as every feeding, or as infrequently as once every 3 days. The key is getting to know what's normal for your baby and noticing if something changes.

Refer back to Chapter 3 for more information about what breastfed and formula poops should look like. Again, this may vary from baby to baby.

Burping

Most babies will need help burping after a feed, but some will burp on their own and need little assistance. The best approach with a newborn is to frequently offer burps before your baby experiences any discomfort.

Over time, you'll figure out a pattern that works for you and your baby. It is important to note that babies will ingest more air if they're crying before a feed, or if they're bottle-feeding.

If you're breastfeeding, start by offering a burp whenever the baby switches breasts. If you're bottle-feeding, burp after every 2-3 ounces, even if they aren't experiencing discomfort. There are specific feeding methods and bottles you can use to prevent your baby from swallowing excess air, but you probably won't need to worry about it. Any air that is ingested during a feed can be relieved by a burp. If your baby is fussy after feeding, this normally means you need to burp them.

How to Burp Your Baby

Generally, gentle circular motions or a soft pat on the baby's back will bring up the bubbles. If that doesn't work though, try wonky winding. Have your baby facing you with their bottom in the middle of your belly button and their head on your right shoulder. Their body should be slightly leaning forward. This places your baby's stomach in the right position to help the air come up and get around the kink in their stomach and esophagus.

Hold your baby tight, so there's light pressure against their belly, and then rub and pat their back.

If you don't like this position or it doesn't work for you, you can also try sitting them upright in your lap, facing sideways, with one hand supporting their chest and chin. From there, rub and pat their back. You may want to try rocking them back and forth while they are sitting on your lap or moving their torso around in a circle or figure of 8 motion.

Don't be obsessed with burping. If nothing comes up and your baby is happy, they probably don't need to burp and it's okay to move on.

Pacifier

The pacifier has become a polarizing topic in motherhood, but whether to use one or not is up to each parent. If you're breastfeeding, it is best to wait until breastfeeding is well-established, around 6-8 weeks, before introducing a pacifier.

The AAP does recommend the use of a pacifier to reduce the risk of SIDS at nap-time and bedtime.[18] Despite some of their downsides, pacifiers are great at soothing fussy babies because sucking is one of the best forms of sensory input and an effective calming mechanism.

To introduce a pacifier, your baby should be calm, not hungry or tired, and swaddled. First, touch their lips with the nipple of the pacifier. If their mouth opens, place the pacifier gently on their lower lip or on the front part of their tongue, and wait for the sucking reflex to start. If your baby doesn't seem to like it, try different shapes and brands. It's also common for babies to have a tongue thrust or slight gag reflex initially.

If your baby settles well with a pacifier, use it from the beginning and don't stress about it. You'll have over a year before you'll need to wean them off of it. It's also okay if your baby wants nothing to do with the pacifier. Offer it for a week and see what happens, but don't force it.

Newborn Cries

All newborn babies cry, but how often, how hard, and how long depends on your baby and will change over time. Most babies will cry for around 2-3 hours a day. Crying all day, every day is not normal.

As long as you're not neglecting them, it's not your fault if your baby cries all the time, but it can leave you feeling immensely frustrated and angry. It's challenging to listen to hours of wailing, especially when you feel helpless.

This is a good time to let your partner or a friend take over for a bit. If you're alone and don't have this option, put your baby down in a safe place, such as their crib, and walk into another room to calm down. Have a breather or a pep-talk, and then pick up your baby when you've relaxed a bit.

Leaving your baby in a crib on their back while you take a 5-10 minute break is okay and doesn't make you a bad mom. Getting angry and frustrated happens to most parents at some point; it's part of being human. Unfortunately, Shaken Baby Syndrome is more common than you might think and happens when a baby's brain is injured from being shaken after a parent or caregiver becomes frustrated. It's better for you to leave your baby in a safe place for a little while than to get angry while you're holding them.

Babies cry for a lot of reasons. They might be:

- Hungry
- Overtired
- Gassy
- Overstimulated
- Bored
- In need of a burp
- Too hot or cold
- Damp (most babies hate being moist or sweaty in their clothing)
- Needing something to suck on, such as a pacifier or finger

It's also possible that your baby is crying for no reason. 2 in 10 babies cry for long stretches, even when nothing appears to be wrong with them. This happens most frequently in the first 3-4 months.[19]

Over time, you'll get better at figuring out why your baby is crying. If you're trying to get your baby to sleep, I like to stick to the 5 S's to soothe a crying baby, as discussed in Chapter 6.

If it's daytime and your baby is crying for no apparent reason, but not due for a nap, first try picking them up. Sometimes, all your baby needs is the comfort of being close to you.

After picking them up, create some movement. This might look like patting their bottom in time with your heartbeat and making a shushing sound. You might rock them in your arms, side to side and forward and backward. You can try the flying superman, bounce on a yoga ball, or put your baby in the baby carrier and move around with them. Walking up and down the stairs can also be great for movement since they love bouncing.

If none of these options work, your baby might like a change of scenery. Try holding them facing outwards instead of facing you, and you might find that having new things to look at distracts them. Walk outside your front door or give them a bath and see if the change in temperature and scenery snaps them out of it. Skin-to-skin contact is another helpful way to calm your baby down.

When all else fails, remember that sometimes babies just cry. If your baby won't settle no matter what you do, you're not alone, and sometimes you have to just wait it out. You are doing the best you can, so don't blame yourself if you can't calm your baby down.

See a doctor if: your baby looks or acts abnormally, such as turning purple, or if your baby cries when you touch, move, or hold them. You should also contact your doctor if your baby cries excessively and won't stop after 2 hours.[20]

Schedules

After your baby is born, you might feel like you need to get them on a schedule right away. Eat, play, sleep is probably the most common schedule you'll hear about from the parenting community. When your little one wakes up from a nap or night sleep, you feed them, play with them, and when the time comes, put them down for sleep again. You'll continue with this pattern throughout the day.

The problem is that scheduling is a modern concept that works fine for some parents, but sets up unrealistic expectations for others. Often, new parents try to follow a schedule and then get frustrated when it doesn't work. This is very normal, because most newborns aren't capable of sticking to routines.

Another issue is that the eat, play, sleep schedule restricts access to the breast for breastfed babies, and can also affect your milk supply.

If you do want to have a daily routine, set one that allows your baby to feed on demand. You might have things you do at certain times each day, but you should let your baby eat before, after, or during these activities.

Author and lactation consultant Meg Nagle said, "Remember your baby is a little human. A little person...and this little person needs frequent breastfeeds and frequent cuddles day and night. You are mothering through breastfeeding...not creating a soldier for the next graduating class of military cadets."[21]

There's nothing wrong with routines, and as adults, we thrive on them! However, there is a time and place for them and they shouldn't be working against you or your baby. If you have a schedule that works for you, great, but if not, it's okay to be flexible and follow your gut and your baby's lead.

Nighttime Routines

Bedtime routines can be helpful, and once your baby hits 8 weeks old, it's well worth focusing on them. They help you and your baby relax, and provide a transition between day and night. Avoid any playtime or other stimulation during your nighttime routine.

You should start about an hour before bed. Many moms choose to begin with a bath, but if it's not a bath night, you can use a warm washcloth and water to clean their face, neck folds, hands, feet, and groin before putting on a clean diaper.

About 40 minutes before bedtime, dim the lights, put on gentle music, and do an infant massage with lotion to calm your little one down. Next, it's time to put on their PJs.

30 minutes before bed, nurse or feed them and 15 minutes before bed, swaddle them and read them a story. Even though they can't understand it yet, reading a story to your baby at least once a day has many benefits. The more words they're exposed to as a baby, the better their language development will be later on.

When it's 5 minutes before bedtime, put your baby down and turn on some white noise where they'll be sleeping for the night.

It also might be helpful to have a nap-time routine, such as dimming the lights, closing the curtains, swaddling and lying the baby down, singing a lullaby, and turning on white noise.

There are so few things we can control as new moms, but having some kind of a routine before naps and bedtime is one of them. It will calm you down and help you maintain your sanity. This isn't to say that your routine won't sometimes be interrupted by a diaper blowout or something else (it frequently will), but you'll still have more consistency in your life.

Playtime

With all of the products available nowadays, it's easy to obsess over entertaining your baby. You will quickly realize that newborns don't do much, but playing with them does help their overall development. It helps them learn about the world and how they can interact with it. It also helps you bond with your baby and get to know each other better.

Playing with a newborn doesn't have to be really involved. It can often be as simple as singing, chatting, tickling, counting toes, playing peekaboo, blowing raspberries on their belly, reading them a nursery rhyme, showing them black and white pictures or patterns, making faces, having them look in a mirror, giving them new scenery to look at, or offering them different objects to feel, hear, and look at.

Color vision will fully develop at around 4-5 months old, so after that, you can incorporate more colors into their playtime.[22] Every new experience with your baby will help them grow. When you're playing, remember to get close to them, ideally 8-12 inches away.

While you're playing, you may notice your newborn looking at you, cooing, or making faces. This is your newborn's way of interacting with you!

Even at a young age, it can be tempting to include screen time in their routine. The AAP recommends children younger than 18 months should not have any screen time other than video chatting.[23] This doesn't mean you can't ever watch an episode of something while your baby's in the room, but do your best to limit your baby's exposure to screens.

Remember, independent play is good for both you and your baby, so don't feel like you always have to entertain them. Studies show that independent play allows kids to foster their imagination, build problem-solving skills, and even helps teach patience and resilience.[24]

Tummy Time

Tummy time is an important part of a baby's development, and the AAP recommends you start tummy time as soon as the baby comes home from the hospital.[25] Good head control and symmetrically developed neck muscles are some of the many benefits of tummy time, so aim to do tummy time at least 2-3 times a day.

You might find your baby resists tummy time at first. The best way to get your baby to like tummy time is to spend more time doing it. In the beginning, start with just 3-5 minutes at a time and get creative. All of these positions can count as tummy time:

- Your baby lying on your chest while you're in a reclined position
- Carrying your baby around the house along your arm while they lie on their stomach
- Burping your baby face down on your lap

When you transition to the floor, try getting down on the floor with your baby so they can see you face-to-face. You can also try placing a mirror or an interesting toy alongside their head. Their neck control will be better with their head to the side in the beginning. If they resist tummy time on the floor, try holding them on a yoga ball instead.

If your baby has reflux, wait at least an hour after eating before tummy time.

Over time, as your baby gets stronger and more comfortable, they will be able to spend longer stretches on their tummy.

Leaving the House

As a new mom, leaving the house for the first time might make you nervous, and that's normal. Even if it's challenging, be confident and assertive in your parenting. I know it's difficult to feel confident when you're a new mom, but remember that you are the parent. If you don't want anyone touching your baby, politely let people know. A baby carrier can be a great way to keep your baby close and minimize other people touching or coughing on your baby.

If you're going out for the day, make sure you plan ahead. Even with planning, trying to get out can take forever. It's easy to start a frustrating cycle: you might decide to feed your baby before you leave so they're not hungry, but now they need a diaper change. By the time you've changed them, they're ready for a nap, so they're wanting to feed again to go to sleep. Now they've spit up on their clothes, so they need to be changed again. This can go on and on, so make sure you build in plenty of time for this sort of thing before you need to leave the house.

Traveling

Believe it or not, you can travel with a baby, but it does take a lot of planning. They don't do much while you're traveling except sleep, eat, and poop, so plan for those three things. Try to coordinate your travel times with their regular nap-times or bedtimes if possible.

Before you travel anywhere, locate a nearby hospital in case of an emergency. Be sure to book a baby-friendly hotel or an Airbnb that has a crib, and think about where you'll do laundry while you're away. It's not recommended for a baby to be in a car seat for more than 2 hours, so plan on making frequent stops if you're going to be on the road.[26]

If you're traveling by plane, here are some tips for traveling with a baby:

- Get to the airport even earlier than you normally would
- Bring a bottle of breast milk if necessary, but be aware that TSA will have to test it[27]
- Bring your stroller with you; you'll be able to gate check it for free
- Feed your baby or play tug-of-war with a pacifier during cabin pressure changes, as this reduces the risk of ear pain
- Bring extra of everything, even if you think you won't need it
- Always have an extra baby outfit in your carry-on, and an extra shirt for yourself in case of spit up, diaper blowouts, etc.

8

Baby Woes

When you picture what life with a newborn will be like, you might imagine the beautiful moments you've seen shared on social media – moments of pure peace and bliss as you soak in that new baby smell and cherish all the newborn cuddles. Don't get me wrong; some moments can be like that, but you probably already know you're also going to face a lot that aren't picture-perfect. Being prepared is a good idea.

One of the hardest parts of having a baby is that they can't really communicate with you. Often, their only method is through crying, and we've already established that crying can mean a lot of different things. Since they can't tell you what's wrong, you need to know what symptoms to look out for so you'll know when you need to get help.

The hard truth is that babies do get sick a lot, no matter how hard you try to keep germs away from them. It's not your fault and it doesn't mean you're a bad mom. An infant's immune system doesn't mature until they're about 2-3 months old. Every time they get sick, they're building the framework that will help them fight off diseases in later life. With that in mind, let's look at what you should have on hand for injuries and illnesses.

First Aid Kit

It's important to have some basic first aid supplies when bringing home a newborn. Here is what your first aid kit should include:

- A thermometer
- Children and/or infant acetaminophen/paracetamol (good for mild pain, generally safe for infants over 12 weeks at approved dosages)
- Children and/or infant ibuprofen (good for pain and inflammation, but AAP doesn't recommend ibuprofen for babies under 6 months)
- Children antihistamines
- Baby gas relief drops
- Saline drops or sprays
- Colorful band-aids
- Baby nail clippers or file
- Tweezers
- Nasal bulb syringe
- Gauze rolls and pads
- Rubbing alcohol swabs
- Petroleum jelly
- Cotton balls

Unexpected Uses for Breastmilk

Breast milk is the perfect food for your baby, but it has benefits beyond nourishment. Leigh Anne O'Connor, an International Board Certified Lactation Consultant, stated, "Human milk is truly amazing. It's like medicine... alive and ever-changing to meet the needs of the baby."[1] Every time your baby nurses, germs from their saliva pass through the nipple, and your body makes antibodies that are then passed back to your baby. Your breastmilk is custom-made to meet your baby's needs.

Breast milk can also be used to heal sore and cracked nipples in between breastfeeding sessions, and to treat minor ailments that your baby may suffer from. It's worth trying on almost any minor problem, including:

- Eye infections
- Ear infections
- Blocked tear ducts
- Teething
- Cuts
- Minor burns
- Warts
- Congestion
- Itching and stinging (e.g. bug bites or bee stings)
- Circumcision healing
- Sore throats
- Baby acne
- Eczema
- Rashes

It may also work as a skin cleanser and skin moisturizer.

To help you prepare for any issue that may come your way during the early days, here are the most common baby ailments.

Blocked Tear Duct

5-10% of newborns end up with a blockage in one or both of their tear ducts. It's normally present from birth, but you might not notice it until your baby is around 1 month old. The symptoms of a blocked tear duct are watery eyes, yellowish discharge, and crusting on the eyes/eyelid.

Most of the time, the blockage will clear up on its own by 1 year of age and doesn't require any other interventions unless it gets infected. To help it along, you can use a warm compress, a few drops of breast milk or a light circular eye massage.

See a doctor if: there's a sign of infection, such as a hard lump that is red or purple near the inner corner of the eye.[2]

Heart Murmur

A heart murmur is an extra sound in the heartbeat. Approximately 75% of newborns have normal heart murmurs that resolve on their own. Anything to do with the heart can seem scary, but your doctor can detect these murmurs by listening to your child's heart, and will determine if it's something more serious.[3]

Physiologic Jaundice

If your baby has jaundice after birth, you might notice slightly yellow skin or yellow whites to the baby's eyes. This is normally noticeable at 2-4 days old.

Jaundice is caused by a high level of bilirubin in the blood. Your baby's liver may not be developed enough initially to remove the bilirubin on its own, meaning higher bilirubin levels after birth are common. There are varying levels of jaundice, so your doctor will determine if any further interventions are needed.

If your baby's levels are particularly high, they may receive treatment before leaving the hospital. For most infants, jaundice goes away on its own within 2 weeks.[4]

Umbilical Hernia

An umbilical hernia is a painless lump in or near your baby's belly button that occurs when a portion of the intestines protrudes through the abdominal muscles. The bulge may only be visible when your baby is crying, coughing, or straining. When your baby is at rest, it should be soft and should push back in easily. If your baby has a large umbilical hernia, it might look serious, which can lead to concerned parents. However, it is usually painless for the baby and doesn't need treatment. Most umbilical hernias heal on their own by the time your child is 4 or 5 years old.

See a doctor if: your baby's umbilical hernia becomes discolored or it's hard and can't be pushed back in. This is considered a medical emergency. Although it is rare, it's something to look out for.[5]

Your Baby's Eyes Look Crossed

Is your baby just making a funny face at you? It's normal for newborn eyes to wander or cross occasionally during the first few months. Their eyes are uncoordinated and can't align to focus on an object, especially close objects, which can result in your baby's eyes being temporarily crossed. Between 4 and 6 months, your baby's eye coordination will improve and their eyes will usually straighten out.[6]

Ear Infection

Ear infections are often dreaded by parents, because even though they're typically not serious, they can be painful.

Ear infections occur when the space behind your baby's eardrum becomes infected and the excess fluid becomes trapped. They're very common and in fact, 5 in 6 children will experience at least 1 ear infection before they're 3 years old.

Parents of little ones who have frequent ear infections can usually tell when their baby has one, based on their level of irritability. The excess fluid in the ear causes pain, so the signs usually include crying, rubbing or pulling at their ear, trouble sleeping, difficulty feeding, ear drainage, or a fever. Some ear infections can resolve on their own, but they can also be treated by a doctor.[7]

White Spots on the Face: Milia

If your baby has white spots on their face, known as milia, they will likely be present from birth. The tiny white bumps might appear on their nose, chin, cheeks, or forehead. These bumps occur when dead skin becomes trapped beneath the surface of the living skin. They may look like white heads, but don't try to pick at or pop them. The bumps will clear up on their own without treatment, usually in a few weeks or months.[8]

Baby Acne

Baby acne might show up around 2 weeks after birth. This condition is found in 40% of babies. It will look like small, red bumps or pustules on your baby's face, scalp, or neck. It has nothing to do with how clean or hygienic you or your baby are. If your baby does have acne, avoid scrubbing, picking, or squeezing it. You may wash it with warm water, or apply breast milk to the skin.

Seeing your newborn with a red, blotchy face may be disconcerting, but baby acne is common and harmless.

See a doctor if: your baby has a fever, or the spots are weeping or bleeding. You should also see a doctor if it doesn't go away by 6 months of age.[9]

Mottled Skin

Mottled skin is a lacy pattern of small, reddish, pale areas on your baby's skin. It's most common on the limbs, but can be present anywhere. This condition is normal for newborns and babies with paler skin, and often appears when a baby is cold.

It's normally nothing to be concerned about and usually happens when there's a lack of blood circulation. Before you panic, check for other symptoms. You can press on their skin and see if the mottled skin disappears for a second. If so, this is a good sign.

See a doctor if: your baby has other symptoms, such as a fever, respiratory distress, dehydration, acting abnormally, or shivering.[10]

Cyanosis

Cyanosis is discoloration of the skin, resulting from poor circulation or inadequate oxygenation of the blood, normally turning the skin blue.

Go to the ER if: your baby's lips turn blue, or the mucus membranes in their mouth or tongue turn blue. This is a sign they're not getting enough oxygen.

Circumoral cyanosis (which creates a blue or gray discoloration only around the mouth as opposed to the lips and inside of the mouth) is fairly common for newborns, but seek medical help if it lasts longer than 48 hours.[11]

Cradle Cap

Cradle cap starts with little patches of dry skin on the scalp, and turns into thick, yellow/white, oily, crusty scales. It's most common underneath their hair, but can also be found behind their ears, on their forehead, in the skin folds of their neck, or even in their eyebrows.

Cradle cap is common in newborns, and although it may be unsightly, it's not contagious and eventually it will go away. There isn't a cure for cradle cap, and it's not a sign that you have done anything wrong.

If you want to help the cradle cap disappear, you can apply an oil, such as coconut oil, at bedtime, and then use a soft bristle brush or silicone brush that's specifically for cradle cap. Each morning or night, gently wash the cradle cap with mild soap to help loosen the scales. Most of all, no matter how tempting it may be, try not to pick it off and be extra gentle to avoid aggravating it.

See a doctor if: your baby's cradle cap is oozing or a foul color, is incredibly itchy, or continues after 3 months of age.[12]

Diaper Rash

Diaper rash is any rash on the skin that's covered by a diaper, and it should always be taken seriously. There are many causes of diaper rash, including chafing, irritation from stool or urine touching the skin for a long period of time, and excess moisture.

Diaper rash usually appears as pink, red, bumpy, or dry skin. In more severe cases, the skin may become raw and bleed, which will be very painful for your baby.

To prevent diaper rash, change your baby's diaper whenever it's wet or dirty. Be extremely thorough and clean any stool out of all skin folds during every diaper change.

During the night, soiled diapers should be changed as soon as you notice, but wet diapers can typically be left till your baby wakes on their own for a feed. However, during awake time, wet or soiled diapers should be changed right away.

Sometimes, wipes can irritate your baby's skin. If this happens, you can use mild soap and water for cleaning. Allow the area to completely dry before putting on a new diaper, and give them some diaper-free time when you can.

You can also apply a heavy layer of diaper rash cream, even before they have a rash, to create a moisture barrier. Ensure that your baby's diaper isn't too tight, especially when they're wearing it overnight.

Usually, a diaper rash will go away after a few days, with a warm bath, warm water washing, lots of diaper ointment, and time for the baby's bottom to air out without a diaper on.

See a doctor if: the rash doesn't look like it's going away, includes blisters or pus-filled sores or if it gets worse 2-3 days after starting treatment.

Yeast/candida rash is a very common diaper rash that will not go away on its own, so you'll need the help of a doctor. A yeast infection rash looks slightly different from other types of diaper rash, and typically has shiny, inflamed patches with defined edges and small, pimple-like bumps.[13]

Other Rashes

Rashes are common in children, and there are lots of different kinds. When your baby has a rash, press on it gently. Does the rash go away? If yes, it's a blanching rash or disappearing rash.

These are not as concerning as other types, but should still be checked out by your pediatrician.

See a doctor if: the rash doesn't go away for a second after pressing on it. You should also see a doctor if it's bleeding or weeping, your baby has a fever, or the rash looks infected.[14]

Eczema

Eczema is a chronic, itchy skin condition. It usually looks like a rough rash that is scaly, red, and patchy. It often goes in cycles: it flares up, and then settles down. It can sometimes be so itchy that when babies are older, it's common for them to scratch themselves to the point of bleeding.

Eczema usually appears in the first few months of life, and babies with this condition have ultra-sensitive skin that loses moisture easily.

The cause of eczema isn't completely understood and it's a complex combination of genetics, environment, immunity, and an altered skin barrier. Over 10% of children have eczema at some point, and about 30% of babies with severe eczema are also allergic to cow's milk and/or eggs.

To help reduce the frequency of flares, give your baby a bath in lukewarm water for 5-10 minutes each night. Always limit the bath to 10 minutes. Immediately after the bath, moisturize your baby. Moisturize as much as you can after every bath, diaper change, and periodically throughout the day. It's important to buy eczema-friendly products, generally labeled as hypoallergenic or for sensitive skin. These products are gentler and help the skin retain moisture.

For severe eczema cases, a topical steroid can be prescribed by your pediatrician.[15]

Thrush

Thrush is a common mouth infection, caused by yeast called Candida Albicans. This infection presents as white or gray patches on the inside of the babies cheek, the roof of the mouth, or on the tongue. You might think it's milk at first, but thrush can't be rubbed off.

Some babies with thrush also develop a yeast diaper infection, or diaper rash. It will look like raised red or purple patches of skin in the folds of their legs and buttocks.

It's common for breastfed babies and their moms to have a yeast infection at the same time and pass it to each other. Thrush can also be picked up in the birth canal. It can be painful and irritating, and will need to be treated by a pediatrician. If you're breastfeeding, the doctor will likely give you something to treat the thrush on your breasts as well.[16]

Hiccups

Hiccups are most common during or after a feeding, and they are normal and painless. Typically, they'll disappear on their own within 5-10 minutes and you can resume feeding. If your baby is getting hiccups all the time, try a different feeding position and only offer a feed when your baby is calm to prevent them from swallowing too much air.

Teething

Teething can begin before 4 months old, or as late as after 12 months. Babies are all different when it comes to teething. Teething can also happen for years on and off as the teeth fully grow. You can usually tell when your baby is teething because they will be drooling constantly, or constantly wanting to chew on something.

To help your baby feel better, try putting pressure on their gums with a finger or teething toy. Cooling can also help, so try letting your baby chew on a cold washcloth (but not a frozen one). Studies have shown that skin-to-skin can help alleviate pain, even among older babies. If you have any concerns or need other ideas for pain relief medication, talk to your baby's pediatrician.[17]

Tongue-Tie

A tongue-tie occurs when the band of tissue under the tongue fails to separate from the tongue before birth. This creates a tightness in the tongue that limits its mobility. Tongue-ties affect nearly 5% of all newborns and are three times more common among boys than girls. Tongue-ties can also run in the family.

Research shows that the majority of infants with breastfeeding problems have tongue-ties, and when they are corrected, these problems are typically eliminated.

Tongue-tie is a relatively simple, quick, and painless procedure. Your baby can nurse immediately after the surgery. However, it may take 30-45 minutes for any numbing medication to wear off.

In most cases, it's up to you to decide if you want to have your baby's tongue-tie taken care of, but it is important to discuss it with your doctor. Leaving a tongue-tie in place can cause other dental or speech issues when your baby is older.[18]

Sucking Problems

The simplest way to check your baby's sucking reflex is to put your finger in your baby's mouth and see if their sucking reflex kicks in. This may be checked by your baby's pediatrician as well.

The sucking reflex helps the baby coordinate the muscles required to drink milk as soon as they are born. This reflex usually develops in the last few months of pregnancy, which means that premature babies might not have had enough time to develop it. This is why premature babies often have to be fed with a feeding tube for the first few days of their lives.[19]

However, this does not mean that sucking problems are limited only to babies born prematurely. There are many problems that may cause babies to have issues with the suck-swallow-breathe mechanism required to feed properly. Some of these problems include infection, nerve damage, brain hemorrhage, cerebral palsy, heart disease, jaundice, the presence of a cleft palate or a cleft lip, tongue-tie, or even medications the mother took during her pregnancy.

Some of the signs that point toward ineffective sucking in young babies are:

- Inability to wake up on their own due to hunger
- Giving fewer than 8 cues or more than 14 cues to feed within 24 hours
- Latch onto the nipple of the bottle but letting go repeatedly
- Pushing away from the bottle and actively resisting latching onto the nipple
- Falling asleep very quickly, either after just 2 or 3 minutes of sucking or 5 minutes after latching on
- Being unable to suck for the first 10 minutes of the feeding session continuously
- Not showing signs of satisfaction, despite having fed for more than 45 minutes
- Excess gassiness
- Producing stools that are frothy or green beyond the first 7 days after birth
- Producing fewer than 6 wet diapers in 24 hours[20]

If it does sound like your baby is experiencing problems with sucking, you should have your baby checked by a Speech-Language Pathologist. If sucking is the issue, they'll be able to work with your baby to enhance their sucking mechanism.

Problems related to sucking don't occur if your baby has been able to successfully feed before or is still able to feed in a sleepy state.

Spitting up vs. Vomiting

It's common for healthy babies to spit up, and it's a rite of passage for many babies. Some babies spit up more than others, and it's normal for this to vary. It's completely painless and they often don't even notice that it's happened.

Spit up happens because their digestive system isn't fully developed yet. Often, it's because they've eaten more than their stomach can hold, or it may happen while they're burping.

It's easy to think they may have spit up their entire feed because it looks like there's a ton on the floor or on your shirt, but it's likely just a few tablespoons. Liquid travels far on clothing and floors, so it may look like more than it actually is.

So, how do you tell the difference between spitting up and vomiting? Spitting up is the easy flow of a baby's stomach contents through their mouth, possibly with a burp. Vomiting occurs when the flow is forceful, shooting out rather than just dribbling from the mouth. Vomiting will also come in a much larger volume.

See a doctor if: your baby is spitting up during the feed, spitting up more than normal, spitting up forcefully, arching their back, or crying. Vomiting can occur from time-to-time for different reasons, but if it starts happening frequently or is bloody or green, consult your baby's pediatrician.[21]

Acid Reflux

Acid reflux in babies is becoming widespread, with around two-thirds of all babies being diagnosed with acid reflux at some point. That's nearly 7 out of every 10 babies![22] Reflux typically happens because the valve between the baby's stomach and esophagus is not completely developed, which can cause the contents of the stomach (including the stomach acid) to rush back up into the esophagus.

Babies who have reflux have a "weaker" esophageal muscle at the top of the stomach. When milk and stomach acid come up through the esophagus, it causes pain and discomfort, and sometimes it comes all the way out of the mouth as vomit.

The valve between your baby's esophagus and stomach will typically get stronger as they grow, which means that the number of babies who suffer from reflux decreases drastically by 18 months of age.

Reflux in babies typically starts before 8 weeks and peaks at 4 months. The most significant improvement will likely occur between 6 and 10 months, when the baby is starting to sit up and eat solids.[23]

Signs that your baby may be experiencing reflux include:

- Gulping or coughing during feeding
- Sudden crying spells during and after feeds
- Projectile vomiting
- Difficulty sleeping or staying asleep
- Screaming while feeding
- Stiffening up while feeding
- Pulling up the legs and arching the back while feeding[24]

Silent reflux is also common and happens when the food escapes back into the esophagus but doesn't make it as far as the baby's mouth. If your baby is suffering from this condition, they likely won't show any obvious signs.

You might hear the reflux while it's happening or notice your baby trying to swallow repeatedly, even when they are not eating.[25]

If you're concerned about reflux, consult your pediatrician for a formal diagnosis and professional advice on the best treatments. Sometimes, they'll prescribe an antacid or special reflux formula for your baby.

There are also some things you can do at home to ease the discomfort your baby is experiencing. Try to:

- Give smaller, more frequent feeds, preventing their tummy from stretching and expanding as much
- Avoid using diapers and clothes that are too tight.
- Keep your baby in an upright position after feeding and avoid putting your baby to bed immediately after feeding
- Burp your baby during and after feeding
- Use paced feeding
- Avoid direct pressure on their stomach[26]

Gastroparesis

Gastroparesis is a condition that occurs when your baby's stomach muscles don't function properly. This can cause the food in the stomach to either leave very slowly or not at all. This typically results in feeling full, nausea, pain, or vomiting.

Unfortunately, the cause of gastroparesis in babies isn't known and there's no cure. Sometimes, the symptoms will subside on their own, but it's also possible that your baby may have them for a long time.

Symptoms of gastroparesis include:

- Getting sick later in the day after a feeding session
- Vomiting foods that have been eaten hours earlier
- Feeling nauseated
- Feeling bloated
- Feeling full after only small amounts of food
- Poor appetite
- Feeling pain or discomfort in the upper abdominal region

If you think your baby may be suffering from gastroparesis, talk to their doctor so they can evaluate your baby and help you come up with a personalized treatment plan. Even though there isn't a cure for this condition, there are medications that help the stomach empty faster, which are typically prescribed to reduce regurgitation. These medications can help manage most of the symptoms, but usually need to be taken long-term.[27]

Cow's Milk Protein Allergy (CMPA) or Intolerance

We mentioned CMPA earlier, but we'll cover it in more detail here. CMPA or intolerance is a common food allergy that occurs in babies under 12 months old and it happens when your baby's immune system reacts unusually to the protein found in cow's milk.

It's important to note that CMPA isn't exclusive to cow's milk. Your baby may also be allergic to other animal milk proteins. Usually, babies with a family history of allergies, eczema, or asthma are at a higher risk of CMPA.

Babies with CMPA may have various symptoms, including reflux, vomiting, nausea, constipation, trapped gas, and excessive farting. If your baby does have CMPA, you'll likely see signs of it during the first 4 weeks of their life.

Some babies learn that they tend to feel sick, bloated, and pained whenever they consume milk, and this causes them to refuse to drink. For many parents, the first sign of this condition is blood in their baby's stool – although you should be aware that there are many causes of blood in the stool, so check with a doctor before jumping to conclusions.

If your pediatrician diagnoses your baby with CMPA, they will likely suggest using a hypoallergenic formula without cow's milk. You don't want to try a hypoallergenic formula before you have an official diagnosis because it is much more expensive and doesn't taste as good as normal formulas, so your baby may drink less. However, if they are allergic, they'll get used to it over time.[28]

Diarrhea

Parents often think their little one has diarrhea when it's just normal newborn poop, which can be very watery. Normal breastfed stools are loose, often runny and seedy, and can even be bordered by a water ring. The best way to tell if your baby has diarrhea is if the number of poops has suddenly increased or they are more loose than normal. Your baby also likely has diarrhea if the stools contain mucus, blood, or smell unusually bad.[29]

Constipation

If you're worried that your baby may be constipated, pay attention to the consistency of their poop, not how often they poop. It's important that their poops are soft and easy to pass, and that they soak into the diaper. Even if they haven't pooped in 2 days, they're not constipated as long as their poop is soft.

Signs of constipation are:

- Dry, firm pellets
- Crying or straining, grunting while pooping (might have a red face)
- Having a swollen belly

Breastfed babies are rarely constipated because breast milk contains a natural laxative, but formula-fed babies may experience this. Some types of formula tend to be more constipating for some babies than others. It's important to make sure you're using the right ratio of water to formula to prevent constipation.

It's almost inevitable that babies will get constipated when you first introduce them to solid foods, but many other things can cause constipation, including types of formula, medication, or sickness (e.g. cold or flu) causing your baby to drink less.

If your baby is constipated, you can try some home remedies to offer them relief. Massaging their tummy in a clockwise direction, moving the baby's legs in a bicycle motion, and giving your baby a warm bath are all ways to alleviate the discomfort.

See a doctor if: the constipation persists, the baby is irritable and has stomach pain, blood in their stool, or a distended abdomen.[30]

Green Poops

As a baby's stool transitions from meconium on days 2-3 after birth, you may see some green stools for a day or two. Next, their poop turns yellow. If your baby is more than a week old, occasionally having green poops isn't a cause for alarm. However, if they're always green, it's likely that your baby isn't getting the fattier part of the milk while breastfeeding and is only drinking foremilk. Foremilk is higher in lactose and harder for your baby to digest. Sometimes, this occurs when you have an oversupply. Talk to a lactation consultant if this is a concern for your baby.[31]

Trapped Wind

Trapped wind is a build-up of gas in the digestive system that puts pressure on your baby's stomach area and causes discomfort. Remember, burps are from eating and farts are from digestion. When your baby swallows a large amount of air while feeding, that should be taken care of right away with burping.

Trapped wind, on the other hand, is caused by the bacteria that line your baby's digestive tract. Signs of trapped wind are often fussiness that is accompanied by arching and squirming. This is usually a sign that your baby is trying to release the trapped air inside them.

To help your baby, you can try movement. Lie your baby down on their tummy across your knees or your forearms and gently massage their back. This method can be more effective than bicycle legs because the pressure on the tummy can help relieve the gas. If your baby is not comfortable on their stomach, lie them on their back and massage their stomach in a circular motion.

If your baby has more severe gas that can't be relieved by movement, you can try gas drops. These drops are dispensed into your baby's inner cheek and will gently break down any gas bubbles in their stomach. You can also use suction devices such as the Windi by Frida. It's a single-use tube that can be inserted into their anus and reaches past the muscle that prevents the release of the gas.[32]

Colic

Colic is when an otherwise healthy baby cries for a longer period than most, and it can last from a few weeks to 4-6 months of age. Colic affects 1 in 5 babies. You can determine if your baby is colicky by applying the 3-3-3 rule: is your baby crying inconsolably for 3 hours a day, at least 3 days a week, for at least 3 weeks? If so, it's likely colic.

No one really knows the cause of colic, but there are some remedies you can try to provide relief and soothe your baby.[33]

First, try burping your baby during and after every feed. If you're breastfeeding, make sure they have a strong latch. You can also try cutting down or eliminating spicy food, caffeine, and alcohol from your diet.

When your baby is fussy, hold them to your chest and let them listen to your heartbeat. Try moving around by swaying or rocking your baby in your arms. You might also try giving your baby a warm bath, a gentle tummy massage in a circular motion, or providing a calming atmosphere with dim lights and no TV.

Colic can be incredibly challenging to deal with. It's exhausting and draining. Do whatever you can to console your baby as long as it's safe, and remember that the crying will stop eventually. Unfortunately, it's typical for these techniques not to work against colic. If you're feeling helpless, reach out to others for support, and keep telling yourself that this phase will pass.

High Needs Baby

A high needs baby is different from a colicky baby. High needs babies are typically more sensitive than other babies, and they also may constantly cry and need extra attention, holding, and soothing. They may have irregular or unpredictable sleep and feeding patterns, and they may be restless, easily overstimulated, and resistant to swaddling.

30% of infants are high needs. You haven't done anything wrong if your baby is among them! While colic will subside at around 6 months, neediness will continue through at least the first year of life. Do your best to meet your baby's needs, but remember that this can be very demanding, so take a break and ask for help when necessary. Like many things in infancy, this is just a phase and your baby will not be this needy forever.[34]

Head Injury

Your baby might have a head injury if they've fallen off a bed, changing table, or other high surface. It's awful to think about, but accidents do sometimes happen. If your baby experiences a head injury, they may have a concussion. Signs and symptoms of a concussion usually show up within 24 hours, but sometimes it can take up to 2 weeks.

See a doctor if: your baby hits their head. Don't take any chances; always take them to the doctor.[35]

SIDS

SIDS stands for Sudden Infant Death Syndrome, and it's a scary idea for many parents. Many parents feel helpless against it because it's not fully understood what causes it. The AAP reported that 3,500 healthy babies die every year in their sleep before reaching the age of 1. Even though you can't fully prevent SIDS, you can greatly reduce the risk by:

- Placing the baby to sleep on a firm, flat mattress. Always place them on their back, even during naps

- Never using a car seat, stroller, swing, infant carrier, or infant sling for routine sleeping. If possible, move your baby after they fall asleep
- Keeping all stuffed animals, soft bedding, pillows, or other blankets away from the crib to prevent suffocation
- Having your baby sleep in the same room as you
- Never exposing a baby to nicotine, alcohol, marijuana, opioids, etc.
- Not overheating your baby. Use the rule of 1 extra (if you're comfortable with 1 blanket, give your baby 2). Babies shouldn't sleep with mittens or hats on
- Avoiding the use of commercial devices that claim to reduce the risk of SIDS. There is currently no known way to prevent SIDS and evidence does not support the use of these devices.
- Give baby supervised, awake tummy time

It is also important to note that pacifiers are associated with a reduced risk of SIDS, and breastfeeding your baby for even 2 months significantly lowers the risk of sleep-related deaths.[36]

Illness: Cold or Flu

When your baby is little, every cough and sniffle will make you worry. Babies get sick very quickly and frequently, but the good news is that they also recover quickly. Whenever your baby is sick, focus on maintaining their hydration. Feeding does often become a challenge when they're not feeling well, and they can become easily dehydrated, so make sure they're drinking enough. You should also keep an eye out for other concerning symptoms and always take them to the doctor if you're worried.

Extra Snotty (Nose Mucus)

Mucus is a lubrication our body makes to keep the nose moist, prevent particles from entering the lungs, and warm the air we breathe in. A blocked nose can make it difficult for your baby to breathe, sleep, and feed. As newborns, babies only breathe through their noses, and mouth breathing doesn't happen until later.[37]

When your baby is extra snotty, do what you can to manage the congestion, especially before a feed. If your baby is very congested, try using saline drops or newborn nasal spray to loosen up thick congestion. First, lay your baby down on their back and slightly tilt their head backward. Dispense 2-3 drops into each nostril. Your baby might sneeze, or snot will run out and you can wipe it.

Suction devices are also an option, but don't get snot happy! These can easily be overdone. The more you suction, the more snot your baby will make. It's best to only use these devices before you feed your baby. Humidifiers can also be a great option for clearing congestion.

Fever

Fever is often a scary word, especially when you have a newborn, but fevers are a normal physiological process and are the body's way of fighting off an infection.

To check a newborn's temperature from 0-6 months, a rectal thermometer is the most accurate method. A nurse or doctor can teach you how to do this and it can be very safe when performed correctly. If you don't feel comfortable doing this, the best next option would be using a thermometer under the arm. Any thermometer will work for this.

See a doctor if: your baby is 0-3 months and has a temperature above 100.4°F or 38°C. At this age, never try to manage the fever at home. Don't mess around: just take your newborn to the doctor or go to the ER if necessary. Newborns are very vulnerable and life-threatening symptoms can be hard to notice. Even if you know it's just a cold because everyone else in the family already has it, still take your baby in.

If your baby is 3-6 months old, check for other symptoms. If your baby has a temperature greater than 100.4°F (38°C), remember that the fever itself isn't dangerous: it's just a symptom of an underlying illness. Parents often get caught up in the number and believe that the higher the fever, the more serious the illness, but this isn't always the case. A child with a temperature of 101.5°F isn't necessarily sicker than a child with a temperature of 100.5°F.

A specific temperature doesn't always equate to an unwell child. However, if your child has a fever and any of the below symptoms, they need medical attention right away:

- They're breathing faster, more noisily, or harder than normal (the skin between, under, or above their ribs is sucking in or they're bobbing their head)
- They're dehydrated: you can tell they're not drinking enough by their number of wet diapers or by dark pee
- They're sleepy, lethargic, or unresponsive (including if their sleep is different from their normal sleep)
- They're in pain and screaming
- They're acting oddly in general
- They're convulsing
- You think they have a stiff neck, headache, or sensitivity to light
- They have rashes

If they don't have any symptoms other than a fever, you don't need to treat the fever or rush to the ER. Focus on keeping them hydrated and comfortable.

See a doctor if: your baby is 3-6 months old and has a fever higher than 102°F (38.9°C). Temperatures can also be too low, and a body temperature below 95°F is considered hypothermia.[38]

Febrile Convulsions/Seizures

A febrile convulsion or seizure is caused by a rapid rise from a normal to a high body temperature. It causes stiffening or jerking movement of the limbs and loss of consciousness. It can last seconds or minutes, but rarely longer than 15 minutes. These are most common between 6 months and 6 years old and typically, your child will be able to breathe through one.

A febrile seizure can be terrifying to watch. When the temperature in the child's body rises rapidly, the brain can't cope. This often happens so fast that you don't even know they have a fever.

There are a lot of misconceptions about febrile convulsions. A higher fever doesn't mean your child has a higher risk of seizures. Febrile convulsions also have not been proven to cause brain damage, and they don't make it more likely that your child will develop a seizure disorder like epilepsy.

Research shows that using ibuprofen to prevent febrile seizures doesn't work. If a febrile seizure is going to happen, you won't be able to prevent it.

Some children will have a one-off convulsion, and some may have multiple febrile convulsions before they grow out of them. If your child experiences one febrile seizure, they have an increased risk of having subsequent ones. There is also a strong genetic link, and future siblings may experience them as well.[39]

If your baby is having a febrile seizure, try to stay calm. Always call an ambulance because you don't know how long it's going to last and it can be terrifying. Lie your baby down on their side on a soft surface. Don't put any medicine or anything else in their mouth, including fingers. Observe what they're doing so you can tell the paramedics when they get there. Look for:

- Lips smacking
- Arms jerking
- Legs jerking
- Eyes flickering

As scary as it may be in the moment, try to focus on what you can control.

When to Go to the ER or Call an Ambulance

Babies always seem to get sick in the middle of the night, so how do you know when to go to the ER or call an ambulance? Especially as a new mom, you might think you're overreacting, even if it is time to get help.

Ask yourself, "do I feel unsafe having my baby go back to sleep while I go back to sleep?" If the answer is yes, go to the ER. Don't question yourself; just go. If your baby is younger than 3 months old and has a temperature of over 100.4°F, go to the ER.

Trust Yourself & Advocate for Your Baby

"Trusting yourself as a new mom is hard. You take classes to learn how to change a diaper and swaddle, but no one teaches you how to be a mom. During my labor, I trusted my doctors and nurses; during my postpartum, I should have trusted myself more. While

Jocelyn Goodwin

in the hospital, my baby wasn't latching, I had a nurse try to "help" and she ended up shoving my 24-hour-old baby's face into my breast. She was crying, which of course made me cry. At that point, I realized that I have to advocate for both of us. From then on, I trusted my mom instincts and knew that what I did for my baby was best because I knew her wants and needs the best. I ended up hand expressing exclusively in the hospital and when I got home, I pumped. We saw a lactation consultant twice a week for 2 weeks until my baby started latching. After that, we had a successful breastfeeding journey and I was able to exclusively breastfeed, even though we struggled with her latch in the beginning."

By Ilana Anderson
Parenting Infants Support Group

Be aware of what's different for your baby, not just what the baseline is for doctors. Trust your instincts. Whether you've spent 2 days or 3 months with your baby, you already know a lot about them. Be confident that you know your child best.

It's not uncommon for a parent to notice something before a doctor does. You may not be a medical professional and you don't need to act like one, but do bring up any concerns with your medical professional. You should be able to trust their diagnoses, but they should also trust your instincts. You know your baby better than a doctor does, so don't be afraid to advocate for them when you know something is off. When it's your baby, the stakes are high.

If the advice you have received doesn't seem right or you feel your concerns aren't being taken seriously, it's okay to ask to talk to someone else or get a second opinion. You will always be your child's biggest advocate. Don't be afraid to step into that role when you need to.

9
Surviving Motherhood

You may have already been told that your life changes completely after having a baby, and it's true. Suddenly, everything in your life revolves around your little one, and although the newborn phase goes by quickly, having a baby means your life is changed forever in all the best ways.

Motherhood is different for everyone, but it does require sacrifice. However, this sacrifice doesn't mean you have to lose yourself entirely. Some people believe mothers give themselves up completely to their babies, while others believe mothers don't have to sacrifice anything. The truth generally lies somewhere in the middle.

A lot of new moms feel like they've lost their identities for a while. It's easy to get dazed by the postpartum bubble, forgetting that life before motherhood ever existed. It's also easy to spend time comparing your postpartum experience with other people's, and worrying that you're doing it wrong. That's why it's important to remember that motherhood isn't supposed to be great all the time, and babies aren't supposed to be happy all the time.

If you're reading this chapter while you're pregnant or during the first few weeks with your baby, then come back and read it again when your baby is 6 weeks old and then again at 3 months old. Set a reminder on your phone if this would help.

Once you've healed from giving birth, you will probably find that you start to neglect yourself and your needs, throwing yourself fully into motherhood. This shows how much you love your baby, but sometimes, you need to step back and make yourself a priority.

Let's look first at why moms tend to lose themselves after having a baby.

Why Most Moms Lose Themselves in Motherhood

There are many reasons why moms lose themselves completely when they become a mom. Sometimes, it's because their career has changed or ended. If your identity prior to becoming a mom was closely linked to your career, it can be easy to start identifying only as a mother, and losing sight of yourself beyond that.

You might stop caring about how you look. This could be because you don't feel great about your postpartum body, or simply because you don't have the time to dress up.

You might be busy but lonely. You'll have zero free time, but you'll probably also feel isolated and bored. You may have a sense of lost freedom since you can no longer socialize, stay up late, or go out with friends whenever you want to.

Lack of sleep can contribute to this, since lack of sleep makes all of us more emotional and less capable of dealing with things. On top of everything, you'll be experiencing rapid hormone shifts. You may be weepy, moody, elated, or irritable, sometimes all at once. You will probably feel overwhelmed, and may be constantly second-guessing yourself.

Almost all moms want two things: to be the best mom they can be, and to nurture themselves. A lot of the time, it may seem impossible to do both, or even one, of these things.

How to Achieve These Two Things as a New Mom

The first step to achieving these two things is to find your new identity. You aren't just a mom whose whole life revolves around your baby. You also aren't the same as the woman you were before birth, who did whatever she wanted, ate whatever she wanted, showered whenever she wanted, and slept whenever she was tired.

You're going through a transition. Embrace it, but be patient with yourself. You are becoming a different person, and you're going to need time to adjust to that.

Most importantly, don't neglect the things that used to bring you happiness. Ask yourself, what did I enjoy before I had a baby? Did I like listening to music? Dancing? Going to the movies? Write a list if it helps.

You might also think about the hobbies you used to have and see how they may fit into your life now. Even socializing might look different, but you can find new ways to connect with your friends and those you love, and you should do so.

The second step to achieving these two things is to realize that you need to make yourself a priority. If you don't, you will quickly discover that failing to take care of yourself means you can't take care of your baby. Of course, this doesn't mean you should neglect your baby's needs every time you favor something different, but you do need to make time and space for yourself in your new, busy life.

Give yourself permission to be at the top of your to-do list. You're the one settling your child to sleep, you're the one being patient, you're the one showing up every day to meet your baby's needs. Being a mom is a tough job, and in order to take care of others, you have to take care of yourself. Focusing on you matters, even if it makes you feel guilty.

Shift Your Mindset

During the newborn phase, everyone will tell you that you need to take care of your mental health, but how do you do that? The following tips will shift your mindset so you can decrease stress, relax, and maximize your energy throughout the day.

Release Expectations

Let go of the idea of how things should be. A lot of us have a sense of what a mom "should" look like, whether that's coming from social media, our parents, or TV. You might feel that there's a lot you need to do to ensure your baby grows up well-rounded and healthy, and those expectations can be heavy.

Try to release them, and let life surprise you. For example, think about your breastfeeding expectations (a common issue). Many moms say they want to breastfeed until their baby is 12 or 18 months old. If that works for you, that's great, but instead of putting a time on it, plan on breastfeeding until it's no longer working for you and your baby. That may be sooner or later than you originally thought – and that's fine.

If you want to introduce a bottle to give your body and mind a break, do. The time with your little one is too short to feel guilty for doing things that make you and your family happier overall.

Another expectation to let go of is that you will sleep when the baby sleeps. That might sound ideal, but it's not always realistic, and you need to be okay with it not working out that way. In short, don't expect too much, and instead just go with the flow.

Feel Every Emotion

Don't suppress your emotions as a new mom. It's an emotional time. You might be grieving for a past you, who had time to shave her legs, put on makeup, and pick out an outfit. You might be longing for the time when you went to bed at 9 p.m. and woke up at 6 a.m. for a morning workout. You might feel guilty about any moment when you're not 100% focused on your baby. You might feel like you're being judged by every single person you know, including strangers on the street.

If you're overwhelmed, cry. If you're frustrated, vent. If you're excited, smile. It's okay to feel all the feelings as a new mom, and you're likely going to feel them all in the span of an hour, or even a few minutes. Oftentimes, emotions are contradictory. You can feel two opposite emotions at the same time. You may be happy when they finally fall asleep in their crib, but sad because you want to pick them up and hold them.

It's also okay to have negative feelings, so let go of the idea that you should always be happy. It's okay to be angry, resentful, guilty, anxious, or upset. Negative feelings are part of being human, and often, you need the bad to appreciate the good. If we didn't have the bad, we wouldn't know what good times were.

Be Kind to Yourself

One of the most important things you can do is have compassion and patience for yourself. Love yourself as much as you love your baby. The relationship you have with yourself influences the relationship you have with your baby. Remember, "you have to love yourself before you can love someone else."

We are normally our own worst critics, and this is also true in motherhood. It can be hard to stop the endless loop of self-doubt and self-criticism.

There's a lot of talk about body positivity and loving yourself, but sometimes, it's just not realistic. Don't get me wrong; there are absolutely times when you should be telling yourself, "I look great!" but in the moments when you're not feeling your best, practice body neutrality instead.

This means you're not beating yourself up for having the extra pounds from pregnancy; you're just accepting what is and knowing that each day, your body will change as it recovers. Some moms will feel completely back to normal after 6-8 weeks, but it's also very common not to feel your best for a lot longer than that. Take each day as it comes, and be kind to yourself.

It's also important to remember that you just had a life-altering experience, so cut yourself some slack. Between your fluctuating hormones and constantly caring for your baby, it's going to take some time to find your footing. As long as you keep showing up every day for your baby, you're a great mom.

This Won't Last Forever

Remember that each stage of babyhood is temporary. When things seem difficult, tell yourself that the season you're in won't last forever. It might feel like it when you're breastfeeding every 2 hours through the night or sleeping away from your partner, but it will go by quicker than you expect. The worst times with your newborn are always the shortest.

Just when you feel like you've figured something out, something else will change and throw everything out of whack again. Be flexible and roll with the punches.

Show Up as Your Best Self

You might wonder what showing up as your best self looks like as a new mom. It's unrealistic to do all of these things every day, but when you feel down, use some of the following tips to boost your mood and mental health.

Uninterrupted Hot Bath or Shower

Self-care often goes out the window when you have a baby and a house to look after. New parents may prioritize vacuuming over taking care of themselves and their bodies. When we think about it, it seems silly, but at that moment, we're just trying to keep our heads above water.

My number 1 tip when the world is overwhelming is to have a hot bath. If you're not a bath person, take a hot shower, but don't treat it like your everyday shower. Put on some nice music, light a candle, and take the time to wash your hair and pamper your body.

Taking a bath at night and using a fun bath bomb can be relaxing, but it can be done in the middle of the day too. Fit it in whenever you have the time. I guarantee that you will be more relaxed, and the issues that seemed uncontrollable will feel a lot more manageable.

Put Yourself Together in the Morning

In the morning, get dressed nicely. You don't have to put on a ballgown, but put on some cute workout clothes, a nice pair of jeans, or anything else that makes you feel great.

This is especially important if you are a stay-at-home mom, since it's easier to avoid getting dressed and taking care of yourself when you're home all day.

Taking 5 minutes to put yourself together will instantly boost your self-esteem and help you to feel ready for anything the day throws at you.

Go for a Walk and Get Fresh Air

Regardless of the weather or how you're feeling, go for a walk with your baby. Get whatever protection you and your baby need, such as hats, gloves, or sunglasses, and get outside for some fresh air.

We spend a large portion of our lives inside, cooking, cleaning, sleeping, and playing. Often, it feels like a chore to step out of the comfort of our homes – but in the end, even a short walk can greatly improve your mood.

If it's cold, wet, or snowy, get in the car and drive to the mall and walk around with your baby in a stroller. Sometimes, all you need is a change of scenery to turn your day around.

Eat Nutritious Food

Although we all know how important food and water are, these are usually among the first things you'll neglect when you have a newborn. It feels like you never have the time to cook or go shopping.

It might seem impossible, but there are so many options out there today to help you get all the nutritious meals you need without spending hours shopping, prepping, and cooking. There's nothing wrong with having junk food every once in a while, but make sure you're eating nutritious meals as well.

Some of my favorite solutions include getting groceries delivered or ordering a meal kit service a few nights a week. You might think it's not worth the money, but many people find that it is. You'll have more energy and mental resilience if you eat well.

Another tip is to buy extras of non-perishables when you do go to the store. If you have the option to, schedule a cooking party with a friend every few weeks. Doing this ensures that you have lots of frozen food that can be easily reheated, and when you do have time to cook, you can make a double or triple batch and freeze the leftovers.

If you are eating fast food, freezer meals, or ice cream for every meal, it's hard to feel good about yourself. Sometimes, eating a healthy meal makes you feel like you can conquer anything.

Do One Thing That Makes You Happy

As a new mom, it's likely that you'll spend your whole day taking care of your newborn, so it's crucial to recharge your batteries as well.

Try to do one thing every day that makes you happy. To ensure you stick to it, decide what that is going to be either the night before or in the morning. Most importantly, there are no excuses. Once you make that commitment, you have to do it. Short of an emergency, there is no reason you can't find the time for just one activity. Prioritize yourself and do it, whether it's doing your nails, sewing, drawing, dancing, solving puzzles, or reading.

Get Things Done!

When you have a new baby, it can start to feel like nothing ever gets done, especially if you have a child who doesn't want to be put down, even during naps. The following are some tips for getting things done.

Tidy in 10

Even though it may seem simple, this is a trick I use almost every day. When you're feeling overwhelmed because every room in the house is a mess, and the laundry and dishes are piling up everywhere, set a timer for 10 minutes and speed clean.

No matter how tired or exhausted you are, you can do 10 minutes. You may be surprised by just how much you can get done in a short period of time. After the 10 minutes is up, you can keep cleaning if you feel motivated or do another 10 minutes later in the day. It's a great way to manage the stress of a messy house.

Do Hard Things at Easy Times

For some reason, as moms, we always seem to do difficult things at difficult times. If your goal is to stop feeding your baby to sleep, 3 a.m. is not the time to implement this rule. Instead, practice it during daytime naps.

The same is true if you want your baby to sleep in a crib when you were previously co-sleeping. Try this at an easy time, not while your baby is going through a growth spurt, cluster feeding, and teething all at the same time. Once you're making headway in the easy times, move on to the harder times.

You Don't Need to Be With Your Baby 24/7

"Wanting a break doesn't mean you're a bad mum. Being a mum is hard work. Leave the baby with someone trusted and have a couple of hours to yourself. You're then fresh and rejuvenated and less agitated."

By Amanda Thomas
Parenting Infants Support Group

It is always best to spend at least the first few weeks with your baby, but eventually, you will need to be parted for a while. Leaving your baby for the first time is stressful! However, it's important for you and your little one to get used to it. It may allow you to get a much-needed break or have a date night. Meanwhile, your baby will get to socialize with someone new and experience a slightly different approach to everything.

Many new moms feel that they can't leave their baby for any reason or any amount of time. It's common to wonder if your baby will feel abandoned or to doubt whether anyone else can take care of them, but it is healthy for both you and your baby to spend a little time apart. To make the process easier, start small. Plan to leave the house just for an hour and then slowly work up to a full day or night.

Before you hire a babysitter, pay attention to the little things that are second nature to you and write them down so you can tell the sitter about them. For example, think about what you do to calm your baby, or the sleep cues or hunger cues they may need to know.

It's a good idea to invite the sitter over beforehand and cover some of the basics. You might give them a tour of your home, do a diaper change, get the baby dressed, feed them, and put them to sleep. Don't be afraid to write everything down so they have it for reference when you're gone.

Be upfront about your expectations and let them know how often you want an update. Remember, this is your baby and it's okay to tell the sitter how you want things to be done.

When you've been apart for a while, you will come back feeling refreshed and ready to tackle whatever challenges come next.

Seek Help

Everyone tells you to ask for help when you need it, but it's harder than it sounds. You may feel like a burden, but actually, the opposite is often true. People love to be needed because it gives them a sense of purpose. The worst case scenario is that they will say no, which will help you identify your true friends pretty quickly.

When you ask for help, be specific, especially if they don't have children. Tell people exactly what you need.

If you're struggling, start small. Invite someone over to keep you company while you go on a walk or go to the mall with your baby.

You may be surprised at how they will naturally offer to help and get involved.

Next time someone asks to come over and see the baby, ask if they would mind bringing lunch with them. Alternatively, when you have a family member over, ask if they can watch the baby for 15 minutes while you take a shower. Small things can make a big difference.

Check a Box

It seems like moms are either excessive planners or completely spontaneous. Regardless of how you like to live your life, the power of having a list and checking chores off can never be overstated. You will feel very accomplished afterward.

Many people find that writing something down in a planner or calendar reduces the anxiety associated with forgetting it. It gets it out of your head so you can focus on other things.

Some people find lists stressful, so if you're not a fan, consider just writing down 1 or 2 things per day. Choose things you know are achievable. If you're completely overwhelmed, write down something that requires minimal effort, such as taking a shower, getting out of your PJs, or sitting outside on the porch.

When you start to get the hang of motherhood, you'll have time to do more things. The key to not getting overwhelmed by a long list of items you need to accomplish each day is to put the non-negotiable items at the top and then only focus on 1 thing at a time.

Do Less

Our society fosters the idea that we have to always be doing everything for our babies and families, and that we're never doing enough, but your baby doesn't need a mom who is running around, making sure the house is spotless, or setting up every single developmental activity to make sure their baby can speak and walk before other babies. Your baby definitely doesn't need a mom who's trying to keep up with all the Pinterest-worthy playrooms and baby clothes.

What your baby needs more than anything is a mom who is present, relaxed, and engaged. It's easier said than done, but learning how to be in the moment with your baby is the most important thing.

Declutter Often

Getting rid of things is something that many people struggle with. It's even harder when it comes to baby things because they hold so much sentimental value. However, having excess clutter causes stress.

You can either use the one-in, one-out rule or set up a declutter day once a month. If you commit to doing it regularly, it normally only takes about 10-15 minutes each time.

Socializing as a New Mom

Socializing as a new mom is very important, but you can also get burnt out fast. That's why one of the first things you need to learn is how to say no.

When you're trying to socialize, you may end up in a lot of situations you don't really want to be in. That could be family obligations, or meeting up with a friend who brings you down whenever you hang out.

This can quickly cause stress and it's not necessary. Refusing to socialize can be hard, because saying no may hurt some feelings, but it means you are respecting yourself enough to know what's best for you. If you find it hard to refuse outright, start by saying "I need to check and get back to you." This will give you time to construct a "no" and figure out the best way to deliver it.

When you do say yes, select the opportunities that leave you feeling uplifted and not drained. These opportunities won't always present themselves without some effort, so nurturing friendships that fill your cup is important.

Often, people find that their social lives drop off after they give birth. That isn't because your friends have forgotten you, but they may think that you're busy with the baby, and avoid calling or stopping by.

It's up to you to make the effort. The easiest way to make time for something like this is to bring your baby with you. Choose activities that you're doing anyway, such as going to the grocery store, and then invite a friend along. If you're afraid of your baby causing a scene, you're not alone – and it's pretty likely that this will happen at some point. Accept that and go anyway. A true friend won't care.

You might also tell yourself you're too tired to socialize, but try to make plans and stick with them. Face-to-face contact with people outside your immediate family can be enormously therapeutic. You will laugh, smile, chat, and forget about being tired or anxious.

Joining a group is another great way to socialize. Parenting can be lonely and it's not always easy to find people that you connect with, so get to know other parents who are going through exactly what you're going through.

If you don't want to leave your house, there are thousands of Facebook groups out there, all tailored to your different needs as a parent. For example, we would love to have you in our Parenting Infants Support Group on Facebook, where there are many other parents who can help you with every part of your journey.

If online groups aren't your thing, it may be beneficial to find some low-cost parenting classes and activities. Many communities have mother-baby social groups that are free or inexpensive. Check out your local library, community center, or church.

Your community is so important when you're a new mom. Find your "mom tribe" with kids the same age as yours, and you might even end up trading babysitting duties with them.

Lastly, be aware that even though we often think of social media purely as a place to socialize, it can take a toll on your mental health and may be a breeding ground for comparisons and negative emotions. Social media is a big part of many people's lives, and it can be a great way to connect with others, but remembering to detach from it for a few hours can help you stay grounded.

We all show our best selves on social media, and seeing someone's best self right now, with perfect lighting and no stretch marks, might make you feel like you're failing. No one is experiencing your life or your exact situation, so try to be content with what you have, instead of focusing on what everyone else is doing. Comparisons can be incredibly demoralizing, and while it's okay to use social media to connect with other parents, don't turn it into a chore that makes you feel bad about yourself, your baby, or your situation.

"I wish someone had told me that not every baby is the same. Just because one baby does something doesn't mean yours will do it too. ALL babies are different in their own little ways. And that is okay!! I wish society would stop putting so much pressure on us moms to raise perfect children. There is no such thing as a perfect child, just like there's no such thing as a perfect mom. We all make mistakes and learn from them along the way!"

By Kayla Elkins
Parenting Infants Support Group

Jocelyn Goodwin

It took me a long time to learn that it doesn't matter what everyone else is doing; there is no single right way to parent. Choose what works for you and your child, and trust your maternal instincts.

The time you have with your baby will go quickly, so when you're nursing, try to watch your baby or daydream instead of using your phone. You might find that you automatically grab it just to pass the time, and many of us don't even realize how much time we spend on social media. Instead, allow yourself to be present in the moment.

Be honest with yourself and determine whether your time on social media is positive and used for connecting with other moms, or if it is making you feel bad and causing you to compare yourself to others.

Strengthen Your Relationship

Relationships can be tough after having a baby. When everything changes, it can feel like your relationship has changed too. The changes don't have to be negative, but you should intentionally seek ways to connect with your partner. Here are some ways you can strengthen your bond.

Let Dad Help!

It's common to feel like you have to do everything as the mom, especially if you're breastfeeding. However, it's very important for Dad to feel needed as well, and he should get involved so he can strengthen his relationship with his baby. Discuss ways your partner can bond with the baby.

Here are some responsibilities your partner might take on:

- Make doctor's appointments
- Soothe the baby to sleep
- Bathe the baby
- Carry the baby in a carrier
- Massage the baby and apply lotion after a bath
- Do diaper changes
- Engage in play
- Share overnight feeding duties if you are bottle-feeding
- Do the grocery shopping
- Batch cook and freeze meals
- Do the laundry
- Vacuum
- Load the dishwasher or wash the dishes
- Clean the bathroom
- Make the bed
- Be in charge of monthly tasks (paying bills, remembering birthdays, buying presents)
- Read stories
- Feed and walk pets
- Tidy up
- Declutter
- Sit and listen to you vent (this can be one of the most helpful)

Not all dads will instinctively step up and help, so you might want to offer some guidance on what you would find useful. However, remember that it's important to not micromanage when he's caring for the baby. Give instructions and then leave him with the baby to figure it out. He may complain and he may do things differently, but they'll get by, and he'll learn. He might also gain a deeper appreciation for the things you do.

Connect With Your Partner

Healthy relationships take time, work, and intention. If you don't nurture them, resentment can quickly surface. Communication is often said to be the key to a healthy relationship, but you might also find that simply doing something together can make a huge difference.

If you enjoy moving your body, try playing a sport together. If you enjoy trivia, put on an interactive quiz on YouTube or Audible to play at home once a week. Cook a meal together, do a puzzle, or play a game. Get creative, leave your phone behind, and make it fun.

Sometimes, focusing too much on talking leads to complaints and disagreements. Before you know it, you're arguing instead of having a good time. With an activity, you can foster and reignite the feelings you have for one another and remember why you fell in love.

There's a lot of pressure to have date nights, but this can be hard for couples who don't have support, and leaving your baby is hard as well. Try to think of ways you can spend quality time together with your baby present. Consider putting your phones on silent for these. You might try:

- Walk together as your baby naps in their stroller, and get an ice cream
- Watch films as your baby sleeps on you
- If you have a big enough bathtub, bathing with the baby, or having one partner sit on the side
- Make some fancy non-alcoholic drinks that you might normally get at a restaurant, and sit together on your porch
- Go on a scenic drive with your baby and blast your favorite tunes

- Do some window shopping together while your baby naps in their stroller
- Order a pizza and have a game night
- Have a picnic in your backyard

Anything that's outside your normal routine should help to reignite the spark between you.

Practice Gratitude

The newborn days can be some of the hardest times for couples because you often feel like you don't know what you're doing, you're running on very little sleep, and you're emotional. Keeping a score of who is doing more can quickly lead to resentment, even for couples who were doing well before the baby was born.

Try practicing gratitude by saying thank you, using both your words and your actions. You, your partner, and your baby are all doing the best you can. It's hard to remember this sometimes, but intentionally finding things to be grateful for can improve your mood and strengthen your connection with your partner.

Touched Out!

"Touched out" describes a phenomenon reported by many moms, especially moms of young children. It refers to feeling overwhelmed by the constant physical contact that babies and children demand, and not wanting further contact.

It's normal to feel this way and especially common for breastfeeding moms, but it can put a damper on your connection with your partner. Unfortunately, you can't be everything to everyone. Your partner might feel rejected and sometimes even jealous of the baby, which may leave you stressed, frustrated, and guilty.

It has been reported that half of mothers feel "touched" out at some point, and it's also common for your libido to drop in the year following birth. Sex and intimacy are healthy parts of a relationship, and if one or both people go for months or years without desiring physical touch, it can cause a lot of issues in a relationship.

It's important to communicate with your partner about how you're feeling and express that this is just a phase. It's not going to be like this forever.

When you are feeling "touched out," it means you're in desperate need of a break, both emotionally and physically. Seek some alone time, whether it's a few minutes in the bathroom or something like a weekly yoga class. Consider hiring a babysitter once a week if you can afford to.

This may also be a good time to reevaluate your lifestyle choices and decide if they are still working for you as an individual and you as a couple. Those choices may be putting unnecessary stress on your relationship, even if they seemed right initially.

For example, if you refuse to let anyone else watch your baby, this could be doing more harm than good, so let someone else step in. You want your baby to grow up in a household where their parents are getting their needs met, and that means regularly evaluating whether rules are still working.

Professional Help

Approximately 1 in every 10 women will experience postpartum depression (PPD) after birth. You might think, "I love my new baby, so why am I sad?" but PPD can affect anyone, regardless of their bond with their babies.

It's critical that you seek help if you experience any of the following:

- Hopelessness

- Lack of interest in your baby
- Feeling overly sad beyond the first 2 weeks postpartum
- Restlessness
- Guilt
- Worthlessness
- Trouble sleeping, focusing, remembering things, or eating
- Persistent feelings of inadequacy
- Resentment
- Hatred of your new life

PPD is different from the baby blues, which are short-lived and typically end after the second week postpartum. PPD isn't something you can or should push through, so if you think you might be experiencing it, get help right away.[1]

If you're not having these specific feelings but think you would benefit from having someone to talk to, you should still reach out to a therapist. You aren't being dramatic or needy; being a mom is hard, and it's okay to need physical and emotional support.

10
Month-By-Month Guide

One of the joys of having a baby is they're growing and changing all the time. Each month brings a new milestone, and it's exciting to watch your baby learn. Although it is helpful to know what to expect, this can also lead to worry and comparisons, especially if your baby isn't meeting the milestones they're "supposed" to.

Each baby is unique, and some babies hit some milestones earlier, while some reach these milestones later. This is why every developmental milestone chart you look at online is different. It shows that there isn't a one-size-fits-all for how babies develop. Don't stress about milestones, and give your child time to explore things and grow at their own pace. However, if there is a persistent issue, talk to a pediatrician.

Here's a general idea of what to expect each week.

Baby Milestones Week 1

Day 1-2

- Very sleepy, might need to be woken to feed.
- Stomach is the size of a large marble.
- If breastfeeding, they will be consuming mainly colostrum.
- Able to recognize your voice.
- Pooping meconium (thick tar-like consistency, back to dark green, sticky poop, no smell).
- At least 1-2 wet diapers.

Day 3-7

- First pediatric appointment.
- Might not cry much.
- Sleeping a lot (16-18 hours per day).
- Appetite will be strong (waking to eat every 2-3 hours).
- Stomach is the size of a ping-pong ball.
- Able to focus on objects 8-10 inches away from the face.
- Seeing predominantly black, white, and some gray.
- Poop will transition to a mustard yellow color.
- Pee should increase every day till they normalize at 6 or more wet diapers per day.
- Can observe new surroundings.

Reflexes you will see during the first few weeks:

- Rooting reflex: touch your newborn's cheek, lips, or mouth with your finger or nipple, and they will turn their head to face you and open their mouth.
- Sucking reflex: when a nipple and areola are placed deep into your baby's mouth, they will automatically begin to suck.

- Moro reflex: often called a startle reflex. When they sense a loud noise or sudden movement they will throw back their head, extend their arms and legs, cry, and then pull the arms and legs back in. A baby's own cry can startle them and trigger this.
- Stepping reflex: it looks like your baby is taking steps if you hold them upright when their feet are touching a flat, solid surface
- Grasp reflex: place a finger on the infant's open palm and their hand will close around the finger. Trying to remove the finger causes the grip to tighten. Stroke the sole of one foot and you will see their toes curl tightly.
- Tonic neck reflex: often called the fencing reflex. If your baby's head turns to one side, their corresponding arm will straighten, with the opposite arm bent. This reflex will fade before they start to roll over.

Baby Milestones Week 2

- First major growth spurt.
- Giving clearer signs when they are hungry.
- Stomach the size of a large chicken egg.
- Crying has fully kicked in.
- Sleeping 15-17 hours per day.
- Likely that their weight will be back to their birth weight.
- 2-week pediatric checkup.

Baby Milestones Week 3

You will start to feel more confident, or at least more confident than when your baby was born. Congratulations! You have changed around 80 diapers by now, and probably fed your baby over 100 times. You will also be better at decoding your baby's cries and knowing what they need.

- Looking around more and opening the mouth to be fed.
- Learning how to snuggle: they will be able to adjust their posture to accommodate yours.
- Really starting to gain weight.
- Jerky and random movements.
- Finding comfort in your scent.
- Eyes will be able to start following you, but may cross as they try to focus.
- Might show signs of reflux.

Baby Milestones Week 4

- Stomach is the size of a plum.
- Aware of their arms, legs, hands, and feet.
- Might start raising their hands to their face or making tight fists.
- Easily startled and will respond to loud noises.
- Recognizing faces.
- Showing a reflex smile, which is not intentional and is short-lived (for example, while sleeping or passing gas).
- Happy spending short periods (3-5 minutes) doing tummy time.
- 1-month pediatric appointment.

Baby Milestones Weeks 5-8

Your baby has passed the 1-month mark! If you haven't gotten out of the house yet, this can be a great time to try it.

- Likely eating every 3-4 hours.
- Increased head movements: moving their head from side to side, raising their head and chest when lying on their stomach for a few minutes, can hold their heads at an angle of up to 45 degrees

- Movement is smoother, more purposeful, and less random: sucking on their fists, swatting at overhead toys, unclenching their fists and reaching for objects
- Starting to see your baby's personality come through: learning their social smile where they are smiling at you (this lasts longer than a reflex smile and accompanies eye contact)
- Making coos and gurgling noises in response to your voice and expressions or "goo" or "aah" sounds
- Laughing when their belly is tickled
- Starting to drool.
- Tracking objects with their eyes.
- Turning their head toward sounds.
- Starting to recognize familiar objects.
- Identifying their surroundings.
- Can see 12 inches away.
- Starting to detect the brightness and intensity of colors, and showing a preference for brightly-colored objects.
- Duration and intensity of crying might start to taper off.
- Slightly fewer naps during the day (3-5 naps).

Baby Milestones Weeks 9-12

- Might be time to transition out of a swaddle if your baby is trying to roll over on their own
- Fully developed sense of hearing and trying to turn toward you when you make a sound: might shake a rattle while they try to understand where the sound is coming from
- Very curious and responsive to sounds, especially high-pitched tones.
- Eager to explore and learn about new things.
- Starting to understand the function of their hands.

- Might start settling into a schedule and predictable feeding schedule (although this is likely to reverse a few weeks later).
- Feeds will be shorter as their efficiency improves, and you may start worrying that they are not getting enough (pay attention to poops and pees and listen for swallowing).
- Might cry at the breast because they are not hungry and don't want it.
- More active during the day: awake more and not just to feed, so you can read books, sing songs, do tummy time, get outside for a walk, people-watch with them, and tell them what is going on.
- Normally the best weeks for sleep.
- Distance perception improves and the baby can see farther away.
- Hand-eye coordination will improve.
- Preference for textures and sounds.
- Sleeping for around 15 hours per day.
- Able to grasp things and roll over (childproof your house accordingly).

Baby Milestones Weeks 13-16

- Starting to demonstrate hand-eye coordination: they can now bring their hands together, curl their hands in a firm grip, look at them, and taste them.
- Laughing, chuckling, and babbling become favorite activities.
- Able to fully roll over from tummy to back.
- Able to reach with both arms.
- Neck and stomach muscles start becoming stronger.
- Most newborn reflexes start to disappear.

- Able to mimic your mouth movements or copy facial expressions
- Able to hold their head steady.
- Able to recognize familiar faces in a crowd and identify strangers.
- 4-month pediatric appointment.

Baby Milestones Weeks 17-20

- Doubled their birth weight.
- Becoming more vocal, producing varied sounds.
- May start enjoying alone time.
- Can be taught to associate sounds with pictures.
- Starting to discover themselves and may even smile at their reflection in the mirror.
- Developing more muscle strength in their upper bodies

Baby Milestones Weeks 21-24

- Starting to crawl.
- Developed color vision.
- Extremely curious and engaged.
- Touching everything they see.
- Starting to put everything in their mouth.
- Leaning on their hands to support themselves when sitting or can sit up unassisted.
- Rolling and rocking back and forth on their knees.
- Might start to consolidate their sleep at night.
- Using their hands to tell you what they do and don't like.
- Responding to their name.
- Putting vowel sounds together.
- Pushing down on their legs when their feet are on a hard surface.

- Might wake up at night due to teething or separation anxiety.
- Growth is starting to slow down.
- Naps decrease to 2-3 times a day.
- Okay to start introducing solids if the baby shows signs of being ready, but breast milk or formula will still meet all your baby's nutritional needs.
- Sixth-month pediatric appointment.

Conclusion

Well, what did I tell you? Motherhood is one crazy and wild ride! Whether you're nearing the end of your third trimester and can't even bend over to tie your shoes or you're in the trenches, waking up every 3 hours to feed your baby, I know what you're thinking. How will I remember it all? You might even be wondering if you'll remember anything you read – and you've only just finished the book! The answer is you're not going to remember every single thing, and that's okay. That's why I recommend you read the book all the way through and then refer back to it as necessary. I hope that you'll find the answers you need here time after time.

The newborn days will be exciting and exhilarating, and will mark the beginning of a beautiful journey called motherhood. You and your baby will both grow in profound ways. Go in with an open mind, be ready to explore, learn, and, most importantly, discover a whole new kind of love!

Stress and anxiety will follow, but try not to worry about what you can't control. I know it is easier said than done, but trust me: the best moms are never perfect. There will be days when the house

Conclusion

will be a mess, or a diaper will explode mid-event, and you'll find yourself doubting everything. Those are the days when you need to be kind to yourself.

Remember, you can't pour from an empty cup, so love yourself and your body so you can care for your family.

Keep in mind that although you are with your baby all the time, motherhood can be pretty lonely. If you're lucky, your partner will be able to stay home with you and your baby for a while, and you may have family or friends who can support you. However, there may still come a day when you feel lonely and desperate for adult interaction. Do not underestimate how powerful finding a community of moms can be. Whether it's through a local moms group, an online platform, or starting your own group, it's important to have mom friends who understand what you're going through.

If you start to feel like you're not ready to be a mom, rest assured that no one is ever fully ready. So much of becoming a mom involves jumping into the unknown and risking everything for the sake of your new baby.

You don't have to know everything to be a great mom. Trust the knowledge you've gained so far, use this book as a guide, and more than anything, trust your instincts. If you don't know what to do, you're not alone. No matter what you're going through, there are many other moms out there who have walked the same path as you.

Motherhood isn't easy, but it's worth every challenge. Take each day as it comes and soak up all the cuddles, smiles, and love your little one has to give you. I believe in you! You've got this, mama!

If you have any questions or you would like something clarified, feel free to email me at:

jocelyn@thefirst12months.com

I answer every single reader's emails.

If you feel like this book helped you, it would be wonderful if you could leave a review on Amazon. Reviews will help other moms who are feeling anxious or stressed about newborn care and postpartum recovery.

How to leave a review:

1. View *Help! I'm A New Mom* on Amazon.
2. Scroll down to the customer reviews section.
3. Click "Write a customer review" on the left-hand side.

Continuing Your Parenting Journey

"It takes a village to raise a baby."

There's a reason this African proverb gets thrown around so often. When parents have a community to support, encourage, and listen to them, raising a baby is so much easier. Parenting is a challenging experience, and having other parents there to answer your questions, provide new ideas, and let you know you are not alone is invaluable.

That's why we created *The Parenting Infants Support Group*, so parents could get together to share ideas and learn from each other.

We regularly run giveaways, share wins from our readers, and answer all the awkward and difficult questions no one else wants to talk about.

It's 100% free and there are no requirements to join, except for the willingness to connect with, support, and learn from others.

You can join us on Facebook by going to:

www.thefirst12months.com/#facebook

Other Books by Jocelyn Goodwin

Available on Amazon & Audible

Spoons and Solids: The Ultimate Guide to Baby-Led Weaning That Eliminates Rules, Fear, and Stress

Acknowledgments

Teamwork is always at the heart of any significant accomplishment. Although I get to interact with and receive all the kind messages from my amazing readers, I couldn't have done it without the people who helped make this book a reality.

First, I'm extremely grateful to Amy Williams, who was instrumental in bringing the facts and ideas in this book to life.

I would like to thank Sarah Schulze MSN, APRN, CPNP, CLC for her expertise and thorough review of the book.

I am grateful to Exxart for creating illustrations and giving the reader a visual representation.

I want to acknowledge our incredible editor, Jo Lavender, whose efforts made a good book into a great book.

I also would like to thank my family for their support, encouragement, and wisdom.

Lastly, thank you to everyone in the *Parenting Infants Support Group* on Facebook. Your questions, input, and support are invaluable, and I am grateful for such a fantastic community of parents.

Much Love,

Jocelyn

Notes

2. Ouch! Healing and Recovery After Birth

1. *Postpartum period: three distinct but continuous phases.* (2010). Journal of Prenatal Medicine. https://www.ncbi.nlm.nih.gov/pmc/articles/PMC3279173/
2. *What to Expect After a Vaginal Delivery.* (2017, June 16). WebMD. https://www.webmd.com/parenting/baby/recovery-vaginal-delivery
3. *Oxytocin | You and Your Hormones from the Society for Endocrinology.* (2020). https://www.yourhormones.info/hormones/oxytocin
4. Watson, S. (2022, November 7). *Postpartum cramping.* BabyCenter. https://www.babycenter.com/baby/postpartum-health/postpartum-cramps-afterpains_11723
5. Watson, S. (2022, November 7). *Postpartum cramping.* BabyCenter. https://www.babycenter.com/baby/postpartum-health/postpartum-cramps-afterpains_11723
6. *Your Postpartum Recovery Timeline: Week by Week.* (2022, November 2). Verywell Family. https://www.verywellfamily.com/postpartum-recovery-4771494
7. *Your Postpartum Recovery Timeline: Week by Week.* (2022, November 2). Verywell Family. https://www.verywellfamily.com/postpartum-recovery-4771494
8. *5 TIPS FOR PERINEAL HEALING POSTPARTUM.* (2014, August 12). Vagina Coach. https://www.vaginacoach.com/blog/5-tips-for-perineal-healing-postpartum
9. *Your Postpartum Recovery Timeline: Week by Week.* (2022, November 2). Verywell Family. https://www.verywellfamily.com/postpartum-recovery-4771494
10. *The effectiveness of cabbage leaf application (treatment) on pain and hardness in breast engorgement and its effect on the duration of breastfeeding.* (2012). NCBI. https://pubmed.ncbi.nlm.nih.gov/27820535/
11. *Your Postpartum Recovery Timeline: Week by Week.* (2022, November 2). Verywell Family. https://www.verywellfamily.com/postpartum-recovery-4771494
12. Watson, S. (2022b, November 7). *Postpartum hemorrhoids.* BabyCenter. https://www.babycenter.com/baby/postpartum-health/postpartum-hemorrhoids_11708
13. *Everything You Need to Know About Postpartum Poop.* (2022, November 2). Verywell Family. https://www.verywellfamily.com/what-to-know-about-postpartum-poop-4774591

14. *Does Walking Help C-Section Recovery? 10 Tips, Exercises*. (2021, December 16). MedicineNet. https://www.medicinenet.com/does_walking_help_c-section_recovery/article.htm
15. *Going home after a C-section*. (n.d.). Mount Sinai Health System. https://www.mountsinai.org/health-library/discharge-instructions/going-home-after-a-c-section
16. Millard, E. (2022, November 7). *Postpartum sweating*. BabyCenter. https://www.babycenter.com/baby/postpartum-health/postpartum-sweating_11720
17. *Breastfeeding Always Hungry: Does Breastfeeding Make You Hungry?* (2020, August 1). Crystal Karges Nutrition - Registered Dietitian Nutritionist in San Diego, CA. https://www.crystalkarges.com/blog/breastfeeding-always-hungry-does-breastfeeding-make-you-hungry
18. *Kegel (Pelvic Floor) Exercises After Birth: How to Do & When*. (2021, April 26). eMedicineHealth. https://www.emedicinehealth.com/when_to_start_kegel_exercises_after_birth/article_em.htm
19. *What all pregnant women should know about blood clots | Your Pregnancy Matters | UT Southwestern Medical Center*. (n.d.). https://utswmed.org/medblog/blood-clots-after-delivery/
20. *Baby blues after pregnancy*. (2021). March of Dimes. https://www.marchofdimes.org/find-support/topics/postpartum/baby-blues-after-pregnancy

3. First Week With Your Baby

1. Unicef UK. (2022, February 13). *Skin-to-skin contact*. Baby Friendly Initiative. https://www.unicef.org.uk/babyfriendly/baby-friendly-resources/implementing-standards-resources/skin-to-skin-contact/
2. Powwow, P. (2017, May 26). *'Mucousy' babies*. Parents Powwow. https://www.parentspowwow.net/mucousy-babies/
3. *Baby's first 24 hours*. (2022). Pregnancy Birth and Baby. https://www.pregnancybirthbaby.org.au/babys-first-24-hours
4. *How Much and How Often to Feed Infant Formula*. (2022, May 25). Centers for Disease Control and Prevention. https://www.cdc.gov/nutrition/infantandtoddlernutrition/formula-feeding/how-much-how-often.html
5. *Early Breastfeeding Expectations*. (n.d.). Scripps. https://www.scripps.org/sparkle-assets/documents/early_breastfeeding_expectations.pdf
6. *Wet Diapers and Newborn Urine Output*. (2021, July 19). Verywell Family. https://www.verywellfamily.com/breastfeeding-and-wet-diapers-whats-normal-431621
7. *Newborn Poop: Meconium and Beyond*. (2021). https://www.nationwidechildrens.org/family-resources-education/700childrens/2021/07/newborn-poop-meconium
8. South Georgia Medical Center. (2019, April 3). *Your Newborn's Appearance*. https://www.sgmc.org/our-services/obstetrics-labor-delivery/post-delivery/newborn-appearance/

9. editor. (2021, December 9). *Average Newborn Weight*. American Pregnancy Association. https://americanpregnancy.org/healthy-pregnancy/first-year-of-life/newborn-weight-gain/
10. Cummings, R. (2020, February 14). *The Amazing Circadian Rhythms of Breastmilk: Why and When Your Baby is Most Hungry | The Birth Center Sacramento*. The Birth Center. https://www.sactobirth.com/blog/2020/1/8/the-amazing-circadian-rhythms-of-breastmilk-why-and-when-your-baby-is-most-hungry
11. *Vaginal Bleeding*. (2022, January 13). Seattle Children's Hospital. https://www.seattlechildrens.org/conditions/a-z/vaginal-bleeding/
12. *Breast Symptoms-Child*. (2022, January 13). Seattle Children's Hospital. https://www.seattlechildrens.org/conditions/a-z/breast-symptoms-child/
13. *Recommendations for Preventive Pediatric Health Care*. (2022, July). AAP. https://downloads.aap.org/AAP/PDF/periodicity_schedule.pdf
14. Howland, G. (2019, May 24). *How Much Should a Newborn Eat? (Hint: Less Than You Think!)*. Mama Natural. https://www.mamanatural.com/how-much-should-a-newborn-eat/
15. *Wet Diapers and Newborn Urine Output*. (2021, July 19). Verywell Family. https://www.verywellfamily.com/breastfeeding-and-wet-diapers-whats-normal-431621
16. *Safe Sleep for Babies*. (2018, January 9). Centers for Disease Control and Prevention. https://www.cdc.gov/vitalsigns/safesleep/infographic.html
17. *Wet Diapers and Newborn Urine Output*. (2021, July 19). Verywell Family. https://www.verywellfamily.com/breastfeeding-and-wet-diapers-whats-normal-431621
18. *How Much and How Often to Feed Infant Formula*. (2022, May 25). Centers for Disease Control and Prevention. https://www.cdc.gov/nutrition/infantandtoddlernutrition/formula-feeding/how-much-how-often.html
19. Kim Conte, Contributing Writer/Editor. (2022, November 7). *Newborn and Baby Poop*. What to Expect. https://www.whattoexpect.com/first-year/health-and-safety/newborn-infant-baby-poop/
20. *The importance of early bonding on the long-term mental health and resilience of children*. (2016). NCBI. https://www.ncbi.nlm.nih.gov/pmc/articles/PMC5330336/
21. *Newborn Senses*. (n.d.). Stanford Medicine, Newborn Health. https://www.stanfordchildrens.org/en/topic/default?id=newborn-senses-90-P02631
22. *Clinical Usefulness of Maternal Odor in Newborns: Soothing and Feeding Preparatory Responses*. (2007). NCBI. https://www.ncbi.nlm.nih.gov/pmc/articles/PMC2046216/
23. *Newborn Senses*. (n.d.). Stanford Medicine, Newborn Health. https://www.stanfordchildrens.org/en/topic/default?id=newborn-senses-90-P02631
24. Navsaria. (2020). *Bathing Your Baby*. HealthyChildren.org. https://www.healthychildren.org/English/ages-stages/baby/bathing-skin-care/Pages/Bathing-Your-Newborn.aspx
25. *Sleep-Related Infant Deaths: Updated 2022 Recommendations for Reducing Infant Deaths in the Sleep Environment*. (2022). AAP. https://

publications.aap.org/pediatrics/article/150/1/e2022057990/188304/
Sleep-Related-Infant-Deaths-Updated-2022

4. Secrets to Successful Breastfeeding

1. *A concise history of infant formula (twists and turns included).* (2020, November 13). Contemporary Pediatrics. https://www. contemporarypediatrics.com/view/concise-history-infant-formula-twists-and-turns-included
2. Wang, Z. (2021, March 24). *The effectiveness of the laid-back position on lactation-related nipple problems and comfort: a meta-analysis - BMC Pregnancy and Childbirth.* BioMed Central. https://bmcpregnancychildbirth. biomedcentral.com/articles/10.1186/s12884-021-03714-8
3. *Positioning.* (2020, August 6). La Leche League International. https://www. llli.org/breastfeeding-info/positioning/
4. *To Hat or Not To Hat.* (2021, February 25). Birthways Family Birth Center. https://birthwaysfamily.com/2019/01/to-hat-or-not-to-hat/
5. *Potential predictors of nipple trauma from an in-home breastfeeding programme: A cross-sectional study.* (2016, August). pubmed.ncbi. https:// pubmed.ncbi.nlm.nih.gov/26895966/
6. *What To Know About DMER (Dysphoric Milk Ejection Reflex).* (n.d.). Motherlove Herbal Company. https://www.motherlove.com/blogs/all/what-to-know-about-dmer-or-dysphoric-milk-ejection-reflex
7. *Breastfeeding and vasospasm.* (2021, June 13). Sprouting Sprogs. https:// www.sarahbrinkworth.co.uk/post/breastfeeding-and-vasospasm
8. Brown, L. C. (2021, April 12). *Managing plugged ducts, mastitis when breastfeeding.* Mayo Clinic Health System. https://www. mayoclinichealthsystem.org/hometown-health/speaking-of-health/ managing-plugged-ducts-mastitis-when-breastfeeding
9. *New Strategies For Relieving Engorgement: Tips and Tools From Maya Bolman, BA, BSN, IBCLC.* (2016, January 26). Lactation Matters. https:// lactationmatters.org/2014/12/08/new-strategies-for-relieving-engorgement-tips-and-tools-from-maya-bolman-ba-bsn-ibclc/
10. NHS website. (2022, September 12). *Breastfeeding and thrush.* nhs.uk. https://www.nhs.uk/conditions/baby/breastfeeding-and-bottle-feeding/ breastfeeding-problems/thrush/
11. NHS website. (2021, November 18). *Tongue-tie.* nhs.uk. https://www.nhs.uk/ conditions/tongue-tie/
12. *Causes of a Low Breast Milk Supply and What You Can Do About It.* (2022, January 26). Verywell Family. https://www.verywellfamily.com/common-causes-of-low-breast-milk-supply-431846

5. No Nonsense Bottle-feeding

1. *Results: Breastfeeding Rates.* (2022, August 1). Centers for Disease Control and Prevention. https://www.cdc.gov/breastfeeding/data/nis_data/results.html

2. *USDA COMMODITY REQUIREMENTS IFD3 INFANT FORMULA.* (n.d.). https://www.fsa.usda.gov/Internet/FSA_File/ifd3.pdf

3. *How Much and How Often to Feed Infant Formula.* (2022, May 25). Centers for Disease Control and Prevention. https://www.cdc.gov/nutrition/infantandtoddlernutrition/formula-feeding/how-much-how-often.html

4. *Amount and Schedule of Baby Formula Feedings.* (2022). HealthyChildren.org. https://www.healthychildren.org/English/ages-stages/baby/formula-feeding/Pages/Amount-and-Schedule-of-Formula-Feedings.aspx

5. *Should You Sterilize Your Baby's Bottles?* (2007, April 12). WebMD. https://www.webmd.com/parenting/baby/should-you-sterilize-your-babys-bottles

6. Choices, N. (2018, March 12). *Can I Use Bottled Water to Make Up Baby / Infant Formula?* Pediatric Safety. https://pediatricsafety.net/2014/08/bottled-infant-formula/

7. *Bottle Feeding Formula Preparation.* (2021). https://www.nationwidechildrens.org/family-resources-education/health-wellness-and-safety-resources/helping-hands/bottle-feeding-formula-preparation

8. Gordon, S. (2020, November 18). *Breast-Fed Babies Know When to Say When.* HealthDay. https://consumer.healthday.com/women-s-health-information-34/breast-feeding-news-82/breast-fed-babies-know-when-to-say-when-638911.html.

9. *Raise a healthy child who is a joy to feed.* Ellyn Satter Institute. (n.d.). https://www.ellynsatterinstitute.org/how-to-feed/the-division-of-responsibility-in-feeding/.

10. Fleur. (2010, December 10). *Baby-led Bottle Feeding.* Nurtured Child. http://blog.nurturedchild.ca/index.php/2010/12/10/baby-led-bottle-feeding/.

11. Higuera, V. (2020, August 28). *Here's Why You Shouldn't Prop Your Baby's Bottle.* Healthline. https://www.healthline.com/health/baby/bottle-propping

12. *10 tips for handling and holding a newborn | Your Pregnancy Matters | UT Southwestern Medical Center.* (n.d.). https://utswmed.org/medblog/newborn-holding-tips/

13. Jennifer Kelly Geddes, Contributing Writer/Editor. (2022, November 7). *Formula-Feeding Your Baby? Here's What You Need to Know.* What to Expect. https://www.whattoexpect.com/first-year/bottle-feeding/formula-feeding-baby/

14. *Newborn Reflexes.* (2022). HealthyChildren.org. https://www.healthychildren.org/English/ages-stages/baby/Pages/Newborn-Reflexes.aspx

15. *Bottle-Feeding (Formula) Questions.* (2022, September 18). Seattle Children's Hospital. https://www.seattlechildrens.org/conditions/a-z/bottle-

feeding-formula-questions

16. *Cows' Milk Protein Allergy (CMPA) and Breastfeeding.* (2019, September 20). The Breastfeeding Network. https://www.breastfeedingnetwork.org.uk/cows-milk-protein-allergy-cmpa-and-breastfeeding/

17. Zimmels, S. (2019, July 3). *Overcoming Feeding Difficulties in Babies with Cow's Milk Protein Allergy.* My Allergy Kitchen. https://www.myallergykitchen.com/overcoming-feeding-difficulties-cows-milk-protein-allergy/.

18. *Selecting Your Bottle Nipple Level.* Dr. Brown's Baby. (2020, March 16). https://www.drbrownsbaby.com/selecting-bottle-nipple-level/.

19. *Selecting Your Bottle Nipple Level.* Dr. Brown's Baby. (2020, March 16). https://www.drbrownsbaby.com/selecting-bottle-nipple-level/.

6. The A, B, Zzzz of Sleep

1. *Safe Sleep for Babies.* (2018b, November 27). Centers for Disease Control and Prevention. https://www.cdc.gov/vitalsigns/safesleep/index.html

2. *Safe Sleep for Babies.* (2018, January 9). Centers for Disease Control and Prevention. https://www.cdc.gov/vitalsigns/safesleep/infographic.html

3. *Mother–Infant Cosleeping, Breastfeeding and Sudden Infant Death Syndrome: What Biological Anthropology Has Discovered About Normal Infant Sleep and Pediatric Sleep Medicine.* (2007). YEARBOOK OF PHYSICAL ANTHROPOLOGY. https://onlinelibrary.wiley.com/doi/pdf/10.1002/ajpa.20736

4. *Parents' Bed – BASIS.* (2022, June 28). Parents' Bed. https://www.basisonline.org.uk/parents-bed/

5. *Co-sleeping with your baby: advice from.* (n.d.). The Lullaby Trust. https://www.lullabytrust.org.uk/safer-sleep-advice/co-sleeping/

6. *What Are Baby Sleep Cues and How to Identify Them.* (2018, April 12). Babywise.life. https://babywise.life/blogs/momtalk/baby-sleep-cues-how-to-identify

7. Karp, H. (2022, June 24). *The 5 S's for Soothing Babies.* Happiest Baby. https://www.happiestbaby.com/blogs/baby/the-5-s-s-for-soothing-babies

8. *Pacifier use and SIDS: evidence for a consistently reduced risk.* (2012). https://pubmed.ncbi.nlm.nih.gov/21505778/

9. *Newborns | BC Children's Hospital Research Institute.* (n.d.). https://www.bcchr.ca/healthysleepforkids/newborns

10. Staff, S. (2019, August 12). *Breast Milk's Unique Composition May Actually Help Babies Tell Day From Night:* ScienceAlert. https://www.sciencealert.com/human-breast-milk-composition-may-help-babies-tell-time

11. NHS website. (2022a, June 1). *Keeping your baby safe in the sun.* nhs.uk. https://www.nhs.uk/conditions/baby/first-aid-and-safety/safety/safety-in-the-sun/

12. The Wonder Weeks. (2022, September 15). *#1 BestSeller - Baby Development Book.* https://www.thewonderweeks.com

13. Gangan, M. (2015, June 5). *REM Sleep Cycle of Your Baby*. Nested Bean. https://www.nestedbean.com/pages/your-babys-sleep-cycle

14. Doucleff, M. (2019, July 15). *Sleep Training Truths: What Science Can (And Can't) Tell Us About Crying It Out*. NPR.org. https://www.npr.org/sections/health-shots/2019/07/15/730339536/sleep-training-truths-what-science-can-and-cant-tell-us-about-crying-it-out

15. Kjær, M. (2017). *Neocortical Development in Brain of Young Children—A Stereological Study*. Oxford Academic. https://academic.oup.com/cercor/article/27/12/5477/3056491

16. *Asynchrony of mother-infant hypothalamic-pituitary-adrenal axis activity following extinction of infant crying responses induced during the transition to sleep*. (2012). Pubmed. https://pubmed.ncbi.nlm.nih.gov/21945361/

17. *Letting Babies Cry – The Facts Behind the Studies*. (2021, June 27). La Leche League GB. https://www.laleche.org.uk/letting-babies-cry-facts-behind-studies/

18. *Night Waking, Sleep-Wake Organization, and Self-Soothing in the First Year of Life*. (2005). NCBI. https://www.ncbi.nlm.nih.gov/pmc/articles/PMC2946618/

19. Bellefonds, C. de. (2022, November 7). *Gentle sleep training: No cry methods, explained*. BabyCenter. https://www.babycenter.com/baby/sleep/baby-sleep-training-no-tears-methods_1497581

7. Newborn Care 101

1. *Car Seats: Information for Families*. (2021). HealthyChildren.org. https://www.healthychildren.org/English/safety-prevention/on-the-go/Pages/Car-Safety-Seats-Information-for-Families.aspx

2. Tanya Tantry, MD. (2020, November 26). *How to Pick Up a Baby: A Step-by-Step Guide for Parents*. Flo.health - #1 Mobile Product For Women's Health. https://flo.health/being-a-mom/your-baby/baby-care-and-feeding/how-to-pick-up-a-baby

3. *Plagiocephaly | Boston Children's Hospital*. (n.d.). https://www.childrenshospital.org/conditions/plagiocephaly

4. *About the fontanelle*. (n.d.). Pregnancy Birth and Baby. https://www.pregnancybirthbaby.org.au/about-the-fontanelle

5. Marcin, A. (2021, November 15). *Guide to Baby Wearing: Benefits, Safety Tips, and How To*. Healthline. https://www.healthline.com/health/parenting/baby-wearing

6. Nicoletti, B. K., Nicoletti, B. K., & Lombardo, B. A. (n.d.). *Baby Carriers: How to Prevent Hip Dysplasia in Infants*. Medtruth. https://medtruth.com/articles/health-features/baby-carrier-hip-dysplasia-in-infants/

7. *The T.I.C.K.S. Rule for Safe Babywearing*. (n.d.). Baby Sling Safety. http://babyslingsafety.co.uk/ticks.pdf

Notes

8. *Umbilical Cord Symptoms*. (2022, January 13). Seattle Children's Hospital. https://www.seattlechildrens.org/conditions/a-z/umbilical-cord-symptoms/

9. Blunden, P. (2021, November 18). *Giving parents the skills to navigate inevitable sickness in kids with confidence and calm*. SICK HAPPENS. https://www.sickhappens.com.au/blog/the-normal-newborn-one

10. Urban, O., MD. (2021, March 18). *Newborn Circumcision Care: Do's and Don'ts for a Quick Recovery*. Flo.health - #1 Mobile Product For Women's Health. https://flo.health/being-a-mom/your-baby/baby-early-weeks/newborn-circumcision-care

11. *What Causes Newborn Vaginal Discharge?* (n.d.). New Health Advisor. https://www.newhealthadvisor.org/newborn-vaginal-discharge.html

12. *Safe Sleep for Babies*. (2018b, November 27). Centers for Disease Control and Prevention. https://www.cdc.gov/vitalsigns/safesleep/index.html

13. *How to Get the Perfect, Safe Baby Bath Temperature for Your Little One*. (2021, May 27). GreenActiveFamily. https://greenactivefamily.com/nursery/bath-time/baby-bath-temperature/

14. Patwal, S. (2015, April 17). *Baby's Hunger Cues: How To Identify Them?* MomJunction. https://www.momjunction.com/articles/common-signs-of-baby-hunger-cues_00350323/

15. Bhattacharjee, D. (2020, August 25). *How to Tell If Your Baby is Hungry - Signs and Age-wise Cues*. FirstCry Parenting. https://parenting.firstcry.com/articles/hungry-baby-knowing-baby-hunger-cues/

16. Sara, N. (2021, January 4). *Dehydration in Babies*. What to Expect. https://www.whattoexpect.com/first-year/dehydration-in-babies

17. Center, L. R. M. (n.d.). *How Many Wet Diapers Should My Newborn Baby Have?* https://www.lanermc.org/community/lane-health-blog/how-many-wet-diapers-should-my-newborn-baby-have

18. Sexton, S. (2009, April 15). *Risks and Benefits of Pacifiers*. AAFP. https://www.aafp.org/pubs/afp/issues/2009/0415/p681.html

19. NCT. (2022, August 18). *How much crying is normal for a baby? | Baby & toddler articles & support | NCT*. NCT (National Childbirth Trust). https://www.nct.org.uk/baby-toddler/crying/how-much-crying-normal-for-baby

20. *Crying Baby - Before 3 Months Old*. (2022, January 13). Seattle Children's Hospital. https://www.seattlechildrens.org/conditions/a-z/crying-baby-before-3-months-old/

21. Nagle, M. (2019, May 10). *Why "Feed, Play, Sleep" routines make no sense for a breastfed baby. . ..* The Milk Meg. https://themilkmeg.com/why-feed-play-sleep-routines-make-no-sense-for-a-breastfed-baby/

22. *Infant Vision: Birth to 24 Months of Age*. (n.d.). AOA. https://www.aoa.org/healthy-eyes/eye-health-for-life/infant-vision?sso=y

23. *Media Use Guidelines for Babies and Toddlers (for Parents) - Nemours KidsHealth*. (n.d.). https://kidshealth.org/en/parents/screentime-baby-todd.html

24. *The Importance of Independent Play*. (2022, May 25). Pathways.org. https://pathways.org/independent-play/

25. Colleen de Bellefonds, Contributing Editor/Writer. (2022, May 25). *Tummy Time for Baby*. What to Expect. https://www.whattoexpect.com/first-year/week-13/tummy-time.aspx
26. *2 Hour Rule | Baby Safe*. (n.d.). https://babysafeltd.com/safety/2-hour-rule/
27. *Breast Milk | Transportation Security Administration*. (n.d.). https://www.tsa.gov/travel/security-screening/whatcanibring/items/breast-milk

8. Baby Woes

1. *Resources*. (n.d.). Leigh Anne O'Connor, IBCLC, LCCE. https://www.leighanneoconnor.com/resources.html
2. *Blocked tear duct*. (2022, February 15). Raising Children Network. https://raisingchildren.net.au/guides/a-z-health-reference/blocked-tear-duct
3. *Heart Murmur in Children*. (n.d.). Children's Hospital of Philadelphia. https://www.chop.edu/conditions-diseases/heart-murmur
4. *Newborn jaundice*. (n.d.). https://medlineplus.gov/ency/article/001559.htm
5. NHS website. (2022a, April 25). *Umbilical hernia repair*. nhs.uk. https://www.nhs.uk/conditions/umbilical-hernia-repair/
6. Wang, A. (2020, February 18). *Why Do Newborns have Crossed Eyes?* Leading Lady Inc. https://www.leadinglady.com/blogs/archive/why-do-newborns-have-crossed-eyes
7. *Signs Your Baby Has an Ear Infection*. (2022, September 28). Verywell Health. https://www.verywellhealth.com/baby-ear-infection-5180874
8. Krupa, A. (2022, May 17). *Milia in newborns*. BabyCenter. https://www.babycenter.com/health/conditions/milia-in-newborns_10894
9. Blunden, P. (2022, February 8). *Giving parents the skills to navigate inevitable sickness in kids with confidence and calm*. SICK HAPPENS. https://www.sickhappens.com.au/blog/the-baby-acne-one
10. Blunden, P. (2021a, January 2). *Giving parents the skills to navigate inevitable sickness in kids with confidence and calm*. SICK HAPPENS. https://www.sickhappens.com.au/blog/the-newborn-skin-one
11. Young, B. (2018, September 29). *Circumoral Cyanosis: Is It Serious?* Healthline. https://www.healthline.com/health/circumoral-cyanosis
12. NHS website. (2022c, August 4). *Cradle cap*. nhs.uk. https://www.nhs.uk/conditions/cradle-cap/
13. *Diaper Rash: Causes, Symptoms, Treatment & Prevention*. (n.d.). Cleveland Clinic. https://my.clevelandclinic.org/health/diseases/11037-diaper-rash-diaper-dermatitis
14. Blunden, P. (2021c, November 18). *Giving parents the skills to navigate inevitable sickness in kids with confidence and calm*. SICK HAPPENS. https://www.sickhappens.com.au/blog/the-viral-rash-one
15. Blunden, P. (2021b, January 2). *Giving parents the skills to navigate inevitable sickness in kids with confidence and calm*. SICK HAPPENS. https://www.sickhappens.com.au/blog/the-eczema-specialist-one

Notes

16. Canadian Paediatric Society. (n.d.). *Thrush.* https://caringforkids.cps.ca/handouts/pregnancy-and-babies/thrush
17. NHS website. (2022d, August 16). *Baby teething symptoms.* nhs.uk. https://www.nhs.uk/conditions/baby/babys-development/teething/baby-teething-symptoms/
18. *Ankyloglossia (Tongue Tie).* (n.d.). Children's Hospital of Philadelphia. https://www.chop.edu/conditions-diseases/ankyloglossia-tongue-tie
19. Eckerle, J. K. (2015, January 14). *Sucking Problems.* Adoption Medicine Clinic - University of Minnesota. https://adoption.umn.edu/sucking-problems.
20. *Difficulty with Latching On or Sucking.* (2019, November 19). Johns Hopkins Medicine. https://www.hopkinsmedicine.org/health/wellness-and-prevention/difficulty-with-latching-on-or-sucking
21. *Spitting up in babies: What's normal, what's not.* (2022, February 25). Mayo Clinic. https://www.mayoclinic.org/healthy-lifestyle/infant-and-toddler-health/in-depth/healthy-baby/art-20044329?reDate=09112022
22. *Reflux in Babies.* Reflux in Babies | Relief | Infant Feeding Problems. (n.d.). http://www.infantfeedingproblems.com.au/en/conditions/reflux/.
23. Shine, R. A. (2020, September 1). *The ultimate baby reflux survival guide - Children's National.* Rise and Shine by Children's National. https://riseandshine.childrensnational.org/the-ultimate-baby-reflux-survival-guide/
24. NHS website. (2022a, January 5). *Reflux in babies.* nhs.uk. https://www.nhs.uk/conditions/reflux-in-babies/
25. *What Is Silent Reflux in Babies?* (2022, July 3). Verywell Family. https://www.verywellfamily.com/silent-reflux-in-babies-5094807
26. Finch, K. (2020, February 17). *Helping Your Baby With Reflux.* Peachymama. https://www.peachymama.com.au/blogs/motherhood/helping-your-baby-with-reflux
27. *Gastroparesis in Children: Boston Children's Hospital.* Boston Childrens Hospital. (n.d.). https://www.childrenshospital.org/conditions-and-treatments/conditions/g/gastroparesis.
28. Zimmels, S. (2019, July 3). *Overcoming Feeding Difficulties in Babies with Cow's Milk Protein Allergy.* My Allergy Kitchen. https://www.myallergykitchen.com/overcoming-feeding-difficulties-cows-milk-protein-allergy/.
29. *Diarrhea (0-12 Months).* (2022, January 13). Seattle Children's Hospital. https://www.seattlechildrens.org/conditions/a-z/diarrhea-0-12-months
30. *Constipation in infants and children.* (n.d.). https://medlineplus.gov/ency/article/003125.htm
31. *Foremilk and Hindmilk.* (2020, August 6). La Leche League International. https://www.llli.org/breastfeeding-info/foremilk-and-hindmilk/
32. Colleen de Bellefonds, Contributing Editor/Writer. (2022b, October 19). *Have a Gassy Baby? What to Know About Infant Gas Symptoms, Remedies and Causes.* What to Expect. https://www.whattoexpect.com/first-year/care/gassy-baby/

33. *Colic.* (2019, November 19). Johns Hopkins Medicine. https://www.hopkinsmedicine.org/health/conditions-and-diseases/colic

34. Higuera, V. (2019, November 20). *What Is a High Needs Baby?* Healthline. https://www.healthline.com/health/baby/high-need-baby

35. *Head Injury in Children.* (2021, August 8). Johns Hopkins Medicine. https://www.hopkinsmedicine.org/health/conditions-and-diseases/head-injury-in-children

36. *American Academy of Pediatrics Updates Safe Sleep Recommendations: Back is Best.* (n.d.-b). https://www.aap.org/en/news-room/news-releases/aap/2022/american-academy-of-pediatrics-updates-safe-sleep-recommendations-back-is-best/

37. Norris, T. (2020, December 8). *How to Treat Nasal and Chest Congestion in a Newborn.* Healthline. https://www.healthline.com/health/newborn-congestion

38. Blunden, P. (2021d, January 2). *Giving parents the skills to navigate inevitable sickness in kids with confidence and calm.* SICK HAPPENS. https://www.sickhappens.com.au/blog/the-febrile-convulsion-one?rq=convulsions

39. Blunden, P. (2021d, January 2). *Giving parents the skills to navigate inevitable sickness in kids with confidence and calm.* SICK HAPPENS. https://www.sickhappens.com.au/blog/the-febrile-convulsion-one?rq=convulsions

9. Surviving Motherhood

1. Carberg, J. (2022, March 22). *Statistics on Postpartum Depression - Postpartum Depression Resources.* PostpartumDepression.org. https://www.postpartumdepression.org/resources/statistics/

Made in United States
Orlando, FL
20 February 2023

30187466R00139